SPEEDBOATS

Sarah Tieck

Big Buddy BOOKS
Amazing Vehicles

ABDO
Publishing Company

Amazing Vehicles

VISIT US AT
www.abdopublishing.com

Published by ABDO Publishing Company, 8000 West 78th Street, Edina, Minnesota 55439.

Printed in the United States.

Coordinating Series Editor: Rochelle Baltzer
Contributing Editors: Megan M. Gunderson, BreAnn Rumsch, Marcia Zappa
Graphic Design: Deb Coldiron, Marcia Zappa
Cover Photograph: *Shutterstock*: Pedro Jorge Henriques Monteiro
Interior Photographs/Illustrations: *AP Photo*: Kevin P. Casey (p. 23), Chris Ison/PA Wire URN:6101355/Press Association via AP Images (p. 25); *Getty Images*: Robert Clanflone (p. 21); *iStockphoto*: ©iStockphoto/dan_prat (p. 15), ©iStockphoto/EnjoyRomania (p. 19), ©iStockphoto/joe32780 (p. 23), ©iStockphoto.com/kirza (p. 7); *Library of Congress* (pp. 29, 30); *Photos.com* (p. 11); *Shutterstock*: AVAVA (p. 15), criben (p. 7), javarman (p. 7), Maciej Karcz (p. 9), Phillip Lange (p. 17), Pedro Jorge Henriques Monteiro (pp. 5, 6, 13, 16, 20, 25, 26) Konstantin Sutyagin (p. 15), Luis Cesar Tejo (p. 23), Zdorov Kirill Vladimirovich (p. 29); *U.S. Navy*: Mass Communications Specialist 2nd Class Kevin S. O'Brien (p. 17).

Library of Congress Cataloging-in-Publication Data

Tieck, Sarah, 1976-
  Speedboats / Sarah Tieck.
     p. cm. -- (Amazing vehicles)
  ISBN 978-1-60453-544-0
  1. Motorboats--Juvenile literature. I. Title.

  VM341.T544 2009
  623.82'31--dc22

                          2009001761

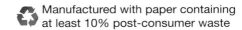

Manufactured with paper containing
at least 10% post-consumer waste

CONTENTS

GET MOVING

Imagine riding on a speedboat. Water splashes as you glide over bumpy waves. You go so fast it feels like you are flying!

Have you ever looked closely at a speedboat? Many parts work together to make it move. A speedboat is an amazing vehicle!

Some speedboats have room for a driver and other riders. Other speedboats are made to carry just one person.

WHAT IS A SPEEDBOAT?

A speedboat is a type of motorboat. Motorboats are vehicles made to travel on water. Speedboats have powerful engines that help them go very fast. They travel on oceans, lakes, and rivers.

Speedboats have different uses. Some are used for **recreation**. Others are used in sports, such as racing. And, some even help people do work.

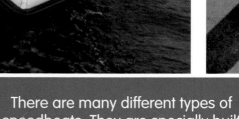

There are many different types of speedboats. They are specially built for how and where they will be used.

A CLOSER LOOK

Many different styles of speedboats exist. But, most have some common features.

All speedboats are built to float on water. Their smooth parts are light, but strong. They must handle rough waters and high speeds. Speedboats are shaped to travel fast!

SPEEDBOATS

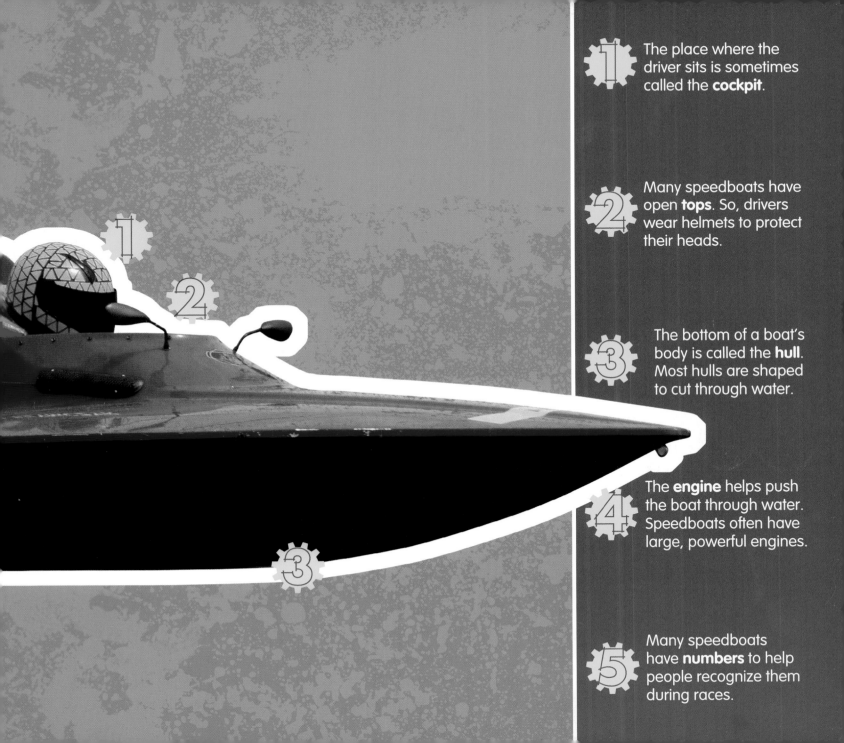

1 The place where the driver sits is sometimes called the **cockpit**.

2 Many speedboats have open **tops**. So, drivers wear helmets to protect their heads.

3 The bottom of a boat's body is called the **hull**. Most hulls are shaped to cut through water.

4 The **engine** helps push the boat through water. Speedboats often have large, powerful engines.

5 Many speedboats have **numbers** to help people recognize them during races.

WHY BOATS FLOAT

Boats float because of density. Density refers to an object's weight and size. Two objects that weigh the same can be different sizes. These objects would have different densities. Objects that are less dense than water will float.

Your body and a stack of weights can weigh the same. But, they are very different sizes. Your body weight is spread out over a larger area. This makes you less dense. The weights are more dense because they take up a smaller space.

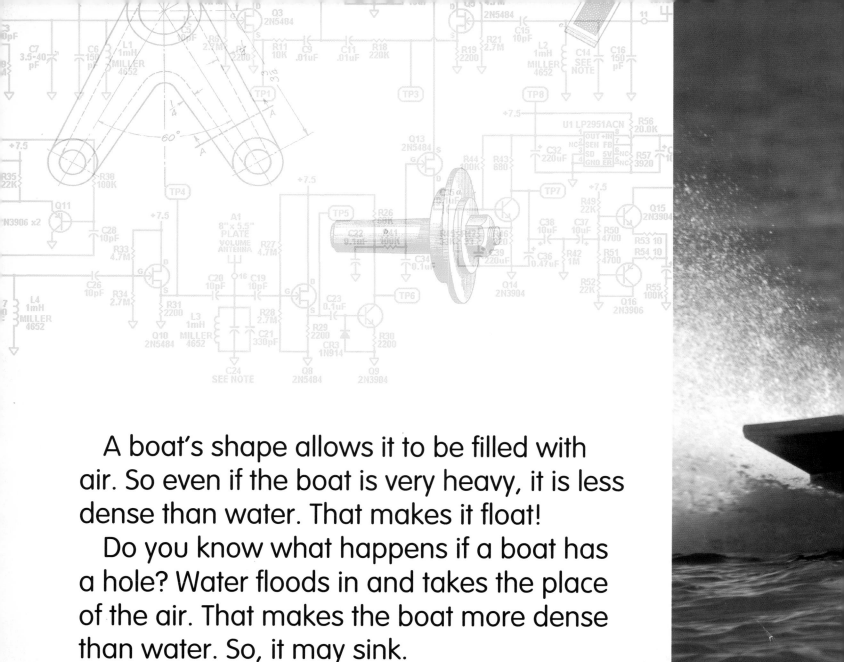

A boat's shape allows it to be filled with air. So even if the boat is very heavy, it is less dense than water. That makes it float!

Do you know what happens if a boat has a hole? Water floods in and takes the place of the air. That makes the boat more dense than water. So, it may sink.

When boats float, they move water out from underneath them. This is called displacement. Very heavy boats displace a lot of water. Light boats displace very little.

HOW BOATS MOVE

A boat's body breaks up water to help it move. Its bow, or front, acts as a **wedge**. When the bow moves forward, it pushes apart water.

But, a boat needs force to help it move. Depending on the boat, force comes from different sources. These include engines, people, and wind.

People paddle with oars to power canoes (*top left*). The wind in sails helps move sailboats (*right*). Speedboats (*bottom left*) are powered by engines.

15

FAST FACT: Some people say speedboats are like sports cars for water. A few speedboats even use engines made by famous sports car companies. These include Corvette and Lamborghini.

A SPECIAL ENGINE

All speedboats have engines. Engines inside boats are called inboard motors. Engines outside boats are called outboard motors. Speedboats can have either type of engine.

A boat engine operates in basically the same way as a car engine. But boat engines are made to move a vehicle in water.

20

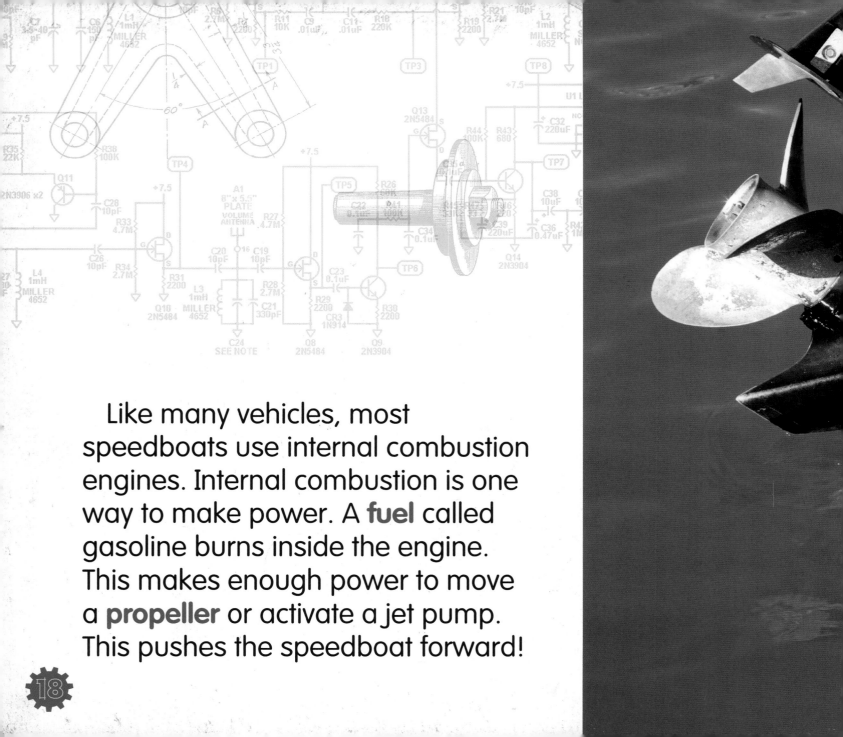

Like many vehicles, most speedboats use internal combustion engines. Internal combustion is one way to make power. A **fuel** called gasoline burns inside the engine. This makes enough power to move a **propeller** or activate a jet pump. This pushes the speedboat forward!

Some boat engines use propellers. Propellers turn, pushing against water. Other boat engines use jet pumps. Jet pumps suck in and shoot out water.

FAST FACT: Speedboat drivers often wear life jackets with kill switches. Kill switches attach to the boat. If the driver falls out, the switch also pulls out. This turns off the boat's engine.

THE DRIVER'S SEAT

Speedboats can be exciting to drive. But, these machines offer little **protection**. So, people driving or riding on boats can get hurt.

It takes skill to drive speedboats safely. In many places, drivers must have a **license** to operate boats. Many people take special safety classes or training, too.

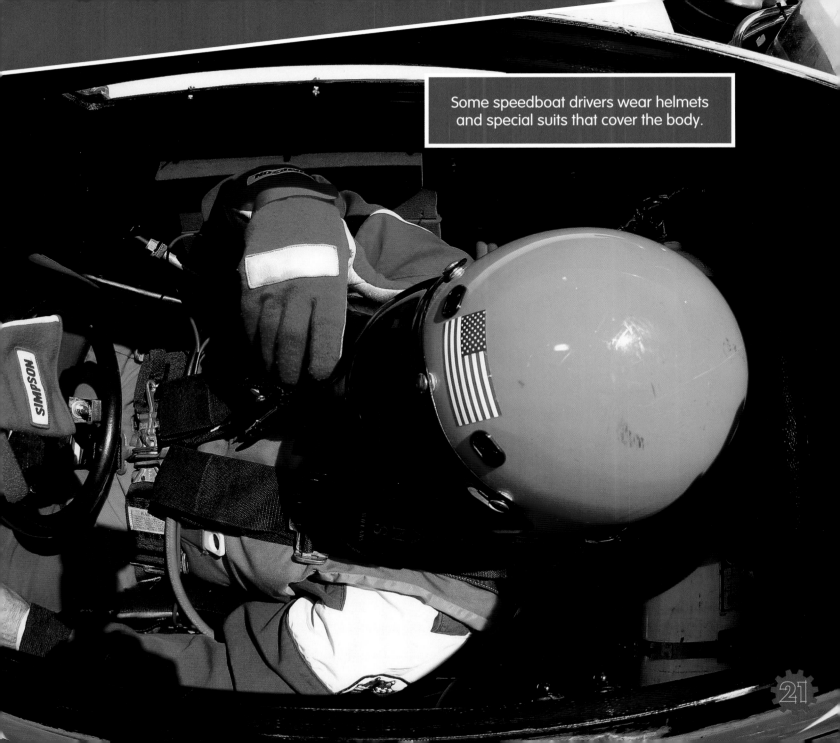

Some speedboat drivers wear helmets and special suits that cover the body.

21

SPEEDBOAT RACER

Some people race speedboats. Many types of speedboats are used for racing. These include hydroplanes, runabouts, and outboard performance crafts.

Many speedboats have special engines made for racing. Some even have two engines. These are called twin engines. Twin engines help speedboat racers go even faster.

Some races are long with many turns. Others are short, straight sprints. Runabouts (*left*), outboard performance crafts (*top right*), and hydroplanes (*bottom right*) are used for different races.

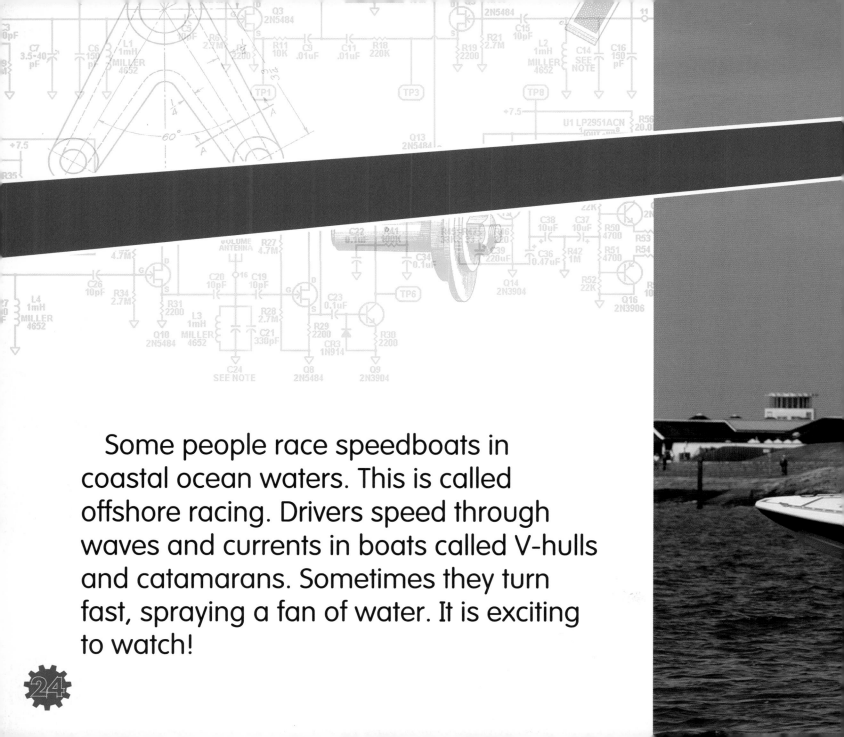

Some people race speedboats in coastal ocean waters. This is called offshore racing. Drivers speed through waves and currents in boats called V-hulls and catamarans. Sometimes they turn fast, spraying a fan of water. It is exciting to watch!

Many speedboat racers use the word stuffing to mean crashing.

There are speedboat races throughout the world. In the Round Britain Offshore Powerboat Race, drivers race for ten days. They travel along the coasts of England, Scotland, Wales, and Northern Ireland.

FAST FACT: Smugglers use speedboats to bring illegal items into the United States. So, the military and the police use their own speedboats to fight this crime.

MILITARY USES

Sometimes speedboats help people with their jobs. For example, military sea forces use them. In speedboats, soldiers can travel quickly through enemy waters. Military forces also use speedboats for daily patrolling and law **enforcement**.

26

Using speedboats to scout for enemies and crimes helps protect soldiers and ships.

PAST TO PRESENT

In 1897, Rudolf Diesel invented a powerful engine. This invention was important for the development of motorboats. As engines became even faster, modern speedboats were invented!

Today, a wide variety of speedboats are used for **recreation** and sports such as racing. And, they help with important work such as military patrols. Speedboats are amazing vehicles!

Speedboats have become fast, modern machines. Today's speedboats have improved engines, shapes, and building materials.

BLAST FROM THE PAST

In the early 1900s, motorboats became popular. And in 1908, they were featured in the Olympic Games! There were three events in motorboat racing.

This was the last time motorboat racing was part of the Olympics. Today, sports that require engines are not allowed. Modern boating events include sailing and rowing.

IMPORTANT WORDS

enforcement (ihn-FAWR-smuhnt) the act of carrying out something, such as laws.

fuel (FYOOL) something burned to give heat or power.

license (LEYE-suhnts) a paper or a card showing that someone is allowed to do something by law.

propeller an object consisting of blades mounted on a bar. An engine turns the bar, which makes the blades spin. This motion moves vehicles such as boats, airplanes, or helicopters.

protection (pruh-TEHK-shuhn) the act of guarding against harm or danger.

recreation (reh-kree-AY-shuhn) an activity done in free time for fun or enjoyment.

wedge something shaped like a wedge. A wedge has two flat sides that narrow to a thin edge.

WEB SITES

To learn more about speedboats, visit ABDO Publishing Company online. Web sites about speedboats are featured on our Book Links page. These links are routinely monitored and updated to provide the most current information available.

www.abdopublishing.com

INDEX

SERIOUS GAMES
FOR THE COLLEGE CLASSROOM

LAW
BUSINESS
ETHICS
SOCIAL
RESPONSIBILITY

Kendall Hunt
publishing company

Donna Clayton

Chapter opener images © Shutterstock, Inc.
Cover image © Shutterstock, Inc.

Kendall Hunt
publishing company

www.kendallhunt.com
Send all inquiries to:
4050 Westmark Drive
Dubuque, IA 52004-1840

Copyright © 2016 by Donna Clayton

ISBN 978-1-4652-8263-7

Printed in the United States of America

CONTENTS

ABOUT THE AUTHOR

Donna L. Clayton teaches business law and ethics in the Bachelor's of Applied Science program at Palm Beach State College, where she is an Adjunct Professor. She teaches The Legal and Ethical Environment of Business and she developed and teaches Business Ethics and Stakeholder Management. Her teaching experience includes executive training programs in Ethics and in Mergers & Acquisitions.

Professor Clayton earned her M.B.A. and J.D. at St. Louis University, St. Louis, MO. She was corporate counsel for United Technologies Corporation for over twenty years, where she served in both aerospace and commercial entities, including as Vice President and Counsel for Carrier Corporation N.A.O. and Vice President and Counsel, Pratt & Whitney Space and Propulsion. She is the founder of the law firm of Donna L. Clayton, P.A., in Tequesta, FL, where she practices corporate law.

Cary A. High is the Department Chair of Paralegal Studies at Palm Beach State College where he also teaches business law courses in the Bachelor's of Applied Science program as an adjunct professor. He has taught and assisted in the development of numerous legal courses including: The Legal and Ethical Environment of Business, Court Systems, Business Law, Criminal Litigation, Administrative Law, and Tort Law.

Professor High is the founder of The High Law Firm, P.A. located in Wellington, FL, where he practices civil and criminal law. Before entering the world of academia and private law practice, Professor High worked as both an Assistant Attorney General and Assistant Public Defender in Fort Lauderdale and Tampa, Florida, respectively. He is an instructor with the Gerald T. Bennett Prosecutor/Public Defender Training Program at the University of Florida. Professor High earned his B.S. in Psychology (with honors) from the University of Florida and continued his studies at UF's College of Law where he earned his J.D. In his spare time, Professor High enjoys spending time with his wife Jenica and his son, Anderson.

Professor High would like to extend special thanks to Professor Donna Clayton for her generosity in allowing him to assist in the production of this text.

PREFACE

Instructors of business law and ethics know that in both the classroom and the courtroom, we tell stories. Stories evoke emotions and emotional connections make "sticky" memories. Jurors remember the virtuous plaintiff or the sympathetic defendant whose characters are revealed through stories, because "sticky" memories transcend the courtroom clutter of procedure and mechanics. Students remember stories of startling injustice and resolute moral leadership when they are emotionally engaged in the outcomes of the stories; these too are "sticky" memories. This text compiles exercises specifically designed to emotionally engage students in the classroom in order to create "sticky" memories.

The exercises in this text are collectively referred to as "active learning exercises." Pedagogical research and analysis has broadly defined "active learning" to include any process in which the students participate actively in their own knowledge acquisition, which can include not only classroom exercises but also internships, model governance programs, and service projects. This text assembles more narrowly focused exercises in which the instructor engages students in the outcomes of the stories by casting them as participants. Even comparatively simple exercises like those in the Chapter 1 "leading questions" format can create memorable suspense and surprise; students who participate in the "hot coffee" exercise will remember for the rest of their lives, whenever they hear the phrase "tort reform," what a third-degree burn from a hot liquid can look like. In more complex exercises such as the simulations and role-plays in Chapters 3 and 4 respectively, the students' involvement and the decisions they make as the stories unfold affect the outcomes of the stories conveyed through the exercises. For example, they may not remember the minutiae of corporate formation alternatives, but they will remember how they felt when one of their company co-founders in the Chapter 3 simulation was accused of stealing; in this example they are forced to make decisions in compliance with their corporate responsibilities, and everyone gets hurt and nobody lives happily ever after. Sticky.

Law and ethics courses are a target-rich environment for storytelling, ready-made with high drama. So why don't we use active learning exercises more often? Two immediate structural impediments discourage their use. First, when we relinquish the podium we relinquish some degree of control over content and time which can threaten curriculum and syllabus commitments. Second, all instructors who have developed and deployed active learning exercises know that they require a substantial investment of time and effort outside the classroom, as well as in it. This text is designed to mitigate these structural impediments. The exercises support specific, enumerated learning outcomes and curriculum requirements. Student preparation materials are provided in off-the-shelf, classroom ready format. In addition, the Instructor's Guide in Chapter 6 provides practical suggestions for launching and managing the exercises, including organization, timing, and grading.

For students: All the exercises are based on real-life legal practice experiences. A business law and ethics class is not law school; to the business management students who are our future business managers, executives, and entrepreneurs, real-world applicability and relevance is essential. The exercises in this text are selected for their applicability and relevance.

For instructors: All the exercises are classroom-tested and are cross-referenced to course outcomes and learning objectives. Unique to this text, the documentation supporting each exercise is "off-the-shelf" to the greatest possible extent, minimizing the burden of customization. The prepackaged materials are consistently accessible by the students and accommodate greater flexibility in their class preparations when compared to *ad hoc* exercises. As mentioned above, the Instructor's Guide includes information for managing the exercises, such as organizing groups, timing considerations, and grading suggestions. Of course each exercise can also be adapted to unique requirements at the instructor's discretion.

The use of active learning exercises in the college classroom will undoubtedly increase, and at an increasing rate. Wired students are accustomed to multi-channel information acquisition and often find it difficult to remain engaged with a one-track podium lecture format. Active learning is interactive and flexibly engages different learning styles other than passive listening. This text is designed, above all, to enrich the students' learning experience. In the author's experience, the instructor's teaching experience will be equally enriched.

CHAPTER 1

Litigation:
Law through the Looking Glass

Donna Clayton and Cary A. High

Chapter Learning Objectives

After completing this chapter, students should be able to:

- Explain how the legal system functions with respect to business practices.

- Discuss laws and legal concepts as they relate to the business environment.

- Use legal reasoning to evaluate case information.

- Use critical thinking skills to extrapolate from the examples to other potential business issues.

> "When *I* use a word," Humpty Dumpty said in rather a scornful tone,
> "it means just what I choose it to mean—neither more nor less."
>
> "The question is," said Alice, "whether you *can* make words
> mean so many different things."
>
> "The question is," said Humpty Dumpty, "which is to be master—that's all."
>
> *Through the Looking-Glass and What Alice Found There* (1871) by Lewis Carroll

Rules of the Game

A legal system serves several purposes. It provides a framework within which social progress occurs at a measured pace. It influences the behavior of public and private entities, corporate actors and individuals, encouraging socially approved conduct and sanctioning unapproved conduct. A legal system also provides a venue for dispute resolution. The American legal system accommodates a variety of dispute resolution alternatives, ranging from the inexpensive and informal voluntary mediation to the expensive, formal, and sometimes compulsory litigation process.

Litigation is usually the most formal, expensive, and final option. Managing any dispute resolution process, including litigation, is similar to managing other business processes: identify the important facts, understand the rules by which the resolution will be reached, apply appropriate cost-benefit analysis to the situation, and make the best decision you can. What's so hard about that?

In this chapter, you will examine three litigation issues which illustrate why litigation outcomes are unpredictable and how traditional cost-benefit analysis may be unreliable when applied to litigation. At the beginning of each example, you will state where you stand on a particular issue based on your own general knowledge. You will then evaluate additional information concerning the issue, which will include reading and video materials. After reviewing the additional information, you will re-visit your position from the beginning of the exercise and state whether your position has changed or not, referencing the specific information which influences your final decision.

> **litigation**
>
> a process for resolving disputes through the courts; in litigation, the outcome is determined by the legal system, not by the principals

CHAPTER ORGANIZATION

Hot Coffee and Tort Reform

Now You See It, Now You Don't: Eyewitness Testimony

White Is Black and Black Is White

Hot Coffee and Tort Reform

Frivolous lawsuits are everywhere. We've all heard about them: the burglar who sued the owners of the home he broke into, because they shot him or he fell through the skylight during the burglary; the psychic who sued the hospital because the CAT scan used in her diagnosis (and to which she consented) destroyed her paranormal powers; the theme park guest who sued Universal because a haunted house was too scary; the woman who sued McDonald's because the coffee she bought there was too hot.

What drives these lawsuits? Obviously, plaintiffs and their attorneys expect monetary gain, but is it possible to quantify these expectations? It's difficult to determine the cumulative effect of such lawsuits in part because many of them are settled for "nuisance" value prior to the filing of publicly available information. In these cases where "nuisance" payments are made, the businesses pay putative plaintiffs to go away, even where the businesses have no liability at all. By doing so, the businesses avoid adverse publicity resulting from the claims; adverse publicity can be damaging even when the business eventually prevails, which most often occurs years after the claims are made if the matter is resolved through litigation. In addition, in the United States legal system as a general rule the parties pay their own legal expenses. Consequently, a settlement might be the best economic solution for a business if the amount of the settlement is less than or equal to the estimated cost of defending the lawsuit even if the business defendant expects to win. In addition, such settlements are often subject to a nondisclosure agreement, which provides further protection for the business.

Federal and state governments have responded to the problem of frivolous lawsuits with a variety of measures collectively referred to as "tort reform." A typical tort reform initiative includes limits or caps on the types amounts of monetary awards a plaintiff may seek in personal injury lawsuits. Tort reform advocates argue that frivolous lawsuits impose excessive and economically irrational costs on businesses. Opponents argue that a blanket limitation or cap is arbitrary and unfairly penalizes a severely injured plaintiff, and the litigation process is already equipped to dismiss frivolous claims by judicial order.

WHERE DO YOU STAND? Assume the role of a business manager trying to decide whether to settle a case or go to trial. Using only your knowledge of business law, common sense, and logic, answer the following questions about tort reform on one page. Do not research the topic. Do not discuss this topic with your classmates. Write from your heart, using your own knowledge and experience.

1. Why are there so many frivolous lawsuits?

2. Imagine you are a lawmaker or a business leader. What measures would you support, if any, to curtail or prevent frivolous lawsuits?

3. What consequences, positive or negative, would you expect from curtailing or preventing frivolous lawsuits?

4. Do we need universal tort reform in the United States?

When you have answered the questions above, form small groups of three to four students and discuss your answers. Select the best answers to represent the consensus of your group. Share your best answers with the class.

MORE INFORMATION

View: "Hot Coffee"[1] A documentary feature film by Susan Saladoff.

THINK AGAIN

Think about the information in the documentary and discuss the following questions and your answers with the class.

1. Does the information in the documentary affect your prior conclusions?

2. Is there anything more you would like to know about the "Hot Coffee" documentary that might affect your conclusions?

3. Can we reach a generally agreed-upon definition of "frivolous lawsuits" for the purpose of public policy discussion?

4. Are there legitimate concerns about unintended consequences of tort reform?

5. Do we need universal tort reform in the United States?

Now You See It, Now You Don't: Eyewitness Testimony

You know it's coming. The witness is on the stand, testifying. He's asked by the prosecution to identify the perpetrator of the wrong. He raises his hand, points toward the defense table and says, with feeling: "That's him. I'm sure of it. I will never forget that face." And jurors tend to find such testimony persuasive.

Now consider a business manager evaluating the litigation option for dispute resolution. Business disputes usually lack the drama that attends lurid criminal proceedings, but when it's your money at stake business disputes can be quite compelling. Perhaps the business entity is a defendant in an employment claim or a negligence claim, and the eyewitness may be called upon to describe a confrontation or an accident. The business litigant must make a cost-benefit analysis taking into account the probability of prevailing at trial. One factor in this decision may be how much weight to give to the testimony of eyewitnesses.

WHERE DO YOU STAND? Assume the role of a business manager trying to decide whether to settle a case or go to trial. Using only your knowledge of business law, common sense, and logic, answer the following questions about eyewitness testimony on one page. Do not research the topic. Do not discuss this topic with your classmates. Write from your heart, using your own knowledge and experience.

1. How much weight would you assign to eyewitness testimony when compared to forensics?

2. Would it matter whether the eyewitness testimony supports or undermines your position in the lawsuit?

3. What additional facts might affect your assessment of eyewitness testimony?

When you have answered the questions above, form small groups of three to four students and discuss your answers. Select the best answers to represent the consensus of your group. Share your best answers with the class.

MORE INFORMATION

View: TEDTalk: Scott Fraser, "The Problem With Eyewitness Testimony," May 2012.[2]

View: "Picking Cotton: A Memoir of Injustice and Redemption" Book Trailer, February 2009. https://www.youtube.com/watch?v=nLGXrviy5Iw

THINK AGAIN

Think about the information in the TEDTalk and the YouTube clip and discuss the following questions and your answers with the class.

1. Does the information in the TEDTalk and the YouTube clip affect your prior conclusions?

2. Are there legitimate concerns about the reliability of eyewitness testimony?

White Is Black and Black Is White

> "I must say that as a litigant I should dread a law suit beyond almost anything short of sickness and death."
>
> —Judge Learned Hand, from "The Deficiencies of Trials to Reach the Heart of the Matter," in 3 "Lectures On Legal Topics" 89, 105 (1926).
>
> Quoted in Frank, Jerome N., "Some Reflections on Judge Learned Hand" (1957). Faculty Scholarship Series. Paper 4099. http://digitalcommons.law.yale.edu/fss_papers/4099.

Litigation risk management anywhere, under any circumstances, is difficult. Litigation by its nature involves a third party. Litigants ask the government, through the court system, to determine the outcome of their dispute. Predicting litigation outcomes with certainty is impossible. In addition to universal litigation uncertainty, the adversarial nature of litigation in the United States introduces another unpredictable element into the process. The adversarial relationship can be particularly toxic, especially to those who are not inured to its impersonal antagonism. Nor is the judge responsible for protecting the tender sensitivities of litigants; in the adversarial courtroom the judge has a less aggressive role, monitoring the process and when necessary acting as umpire. In this system it is the trial attorney who is charged with the zealous advocacy of his client's positions, in support of which he or she advances evidence and arguments that favor the client and diminishes or destroys evidence unfavorable to the client. In an adversarial system the skill of the litigator is a weighty factor indeed. Even when the business litigant has a strong case, that case can be devastated by a skillful litigator who has only one objective—not to find the truth, not to find justice—but to win.

WHERE DO YOU STAND? Assume the role of a business manager trying to decide whether to settle a case or go to trial. Using only your knowledge of business law, common sense, and logic, answer the following questions about the adversarial system on one page. Do not research the topic. Do not discuss this topic with your classmates. Write from your heart, using your own knowledge and experience.

1. Does the adversarial system seek justice or does it seek truth?

2. Does the adversarial system promote procedural due process at the expense of substantive due process?

3. What additional information would affect your assessment of the adversarial system and whether your business dispute would be resolved fairly?

When you have answered the questions above, form small groups of three to four students and discuss your answers. Select the best answers to represent the consensus of your group. Share your best answers with the class.

MORE INFORMATION (PART 1)

View: "Triangle Fire."[3] A PBS American Experience documentary film.

Read: Max Steuer Cross-examination of Kate Alterman, Appendix 1 to this Chapter 1.[4]

MORE INFORMATION (PART 2)

View: Rodney King Beating (full version)[5]

View: News Report on Rodney King Trial (use of video in trial)[6] https://www.youtube.com/watch?v=puElaTZSakw

THINK AGAIN

Think about the information in the Triangle Fire video, the Triangle Fire trial transcript, and the two Rodney King videos, and discuss the following questions and your answers with the class.

1. The Triangle Fire video suggests that the young women working in the Triangle factory were of comparatively low social status; was their social status relevant to Steuer's cross-examination of Kate Alterman?

2. Steuer never accused Kate Alterman of giving false testimony. Procedural due process was never questioned. Steuer took testimony that should have been powerfully persuasive against his clients' interests and turned it against the prosecution instead. Does this affect your prior conclusions about truth and justice in the adversarial trial process?

3. The Rodney King Beating Video (full version) would appear to be detrimental to the interests of the police officers involved in the incident. At trial however, the defense attorneys for the officers showed the video clip frame-by-frame, explaining through witness testimony how the officers perceived the situation. Do you think this defense tactic is similar to Max Steuer's cross-examination of Kate Alterman?

4. Are there legitimate concerns about the potential effect of particularly ruthless and effective trial tactics?

APPENDIX 1

MAX STEUER CROSS-EXAMINATION OF KATE ALTERMAN

Author's Note: The sections of the official transcript pertaining to the testimony of Kate Alterman and the cross-examination by Max Steuer are included below. Students should note that Defendants' counsel, Max Steuer, asks Alterman to repeat her testimony four times. Because the transcript was damaged, some of the testimony was reconstructed and the internal pagination is inconsistent. The entire trial transcript is available online at Cornell University ILR School DigitalCommons@ILR.

The tragic fire of March 25, 1911 at the Triangle factory in New York City was the basis of a criminal prosecution against the factory owners, Max Blanck and Isaac Harris, on charges of manslaughter. The prosecutor, Charles Bostwick, introduced direct testimony of survivors of the fire, who were typically young, immigrant women. Some of the witnesses did not speak English and testified through translators. One survivor, Kate Alterman, testified graphically about the horrific conditions inside the burning building, describing a "curtain of fire" and a man like "a wild cat" at the windows "covered with flames."

Attorney Max Steuer, an exceptionally skillful litigator whose defense in the case is now legendary, represented defendants Blanck and Harris. Rather than moving quickly away from the dramatic and horrible details recounted by Kate Alterman as might be expected, he asked her to repeat her story, saying "Tell us what you did" and she repeated her account in all its lurid detail. Then he said, "Now could you tell us again what you did . . . ?" and she recounted it a third time. He then directed her to a point in the middle of her testimony and said "Now tell us from there on what you did" and she told her story a fourth time.

Conventional wisdom would have suggested trying to minimize the effect on the jury of Kate Alterman's powerful testimony. Steuer did the opposite. Observers present at the trial affirmed the efficacy of Steuer's tactics. His ruthless cross-examination planted a suspicion in the minds of the jurors that her testimony was coached and memorized, and therefore not reliable. Blanck and Harris were acquitted of all charges.

‡ ‡ ‡ ‡ ‡ ‡

Page 1154: Kate Alperman (sic), 9th floor, who worked 4 months, operator.

Page 1155: (These are the long passages for comparison purposes) Was Margaret Swartz with you at this time? Yes, sir. Then I went to the toilet room. Margaret disappeared from me, and I wanted to go out the Greene Street side but the whole door was in flames, so I went and hide myself in the toilet rooms, and then I went outside away from the toilet rooms and bent my face over the sink, and then I ran to the Washington Place side elevator, but there was a big crowd and I couldn't pass through there. Then I noticed someone, a whole crowd, around the door, and I saw Bernstein, the manager's brother, trying to open the door, and there was Margaret near him. Bernstein tried the door; he couldn't open it, and then Margaret began to open that door. I take her on one side, I pushed her on the side and I said wait, I will open that door. I tried, pulled the handle in and out, all ways, and I couldn't open it. She pushed me on the other side, got hold of the handle, and then she tried, and then I saw her bending down on her knees, and her hair was loose and the trail of her dress was a little far from her, and then a big smoke came and I couldn't see. I just knew it was Margaret, and I said Margaret, and she didn't reply. I left Margaret, and I turned my head on the side and I noticed the trail of her dress and the ends of her hair begin to burn. Then I ran in, in the small dressing room that was on the Washington side. There was a big crowd and I went out from there and stood in the center of the room between the machines and between the examining tables, I noticed afterwards on the other side near the Washington side windows Bernstein, the manager's brother, going around like a wild cat on the windows, and he was chasing his head out of the window and pulled himself back. He wanted to jump, I suppose, but he was afraid. And then I saw the flames covering him. I noticed on the Greene Street side someone else fall down on the floor and the flames covered him, and then I stood in the center of the room and I just turned my coat on the left side with the fur to my face, the lining on the outside, got hold of a bunch of dresses that was lying on the examining tables and not burned yet, covered up my head and tried to run through the flames on the Greene Street side. The whole door was a red curtain of fire, but a young lady came and she began to pull me in the back of my dress and she wouldn't let me. I kicked her with my foot and I don't know what became of her, and I ran out through the Greene Street side door, right through the flames, onto the roof. My pocketbook began to burn already but I pressed it to my heart to extinguish the fire. And the last time I saw Margaret Swartz was at the door, she says.

Page 1157: She screamed at the top of her voice, My God I am lost, the door is locked, open the door. That is the last I ever saw of Margaret Swartz.

Page 1161: Now, here she repeats the entire story. Now tell us what you did when you heard the cry of fire? I went out from the dressing room, went to the Waverly side windows to look for fire escapes. I didn't find any. Margaret Swartz was with me. Afterwards she disappeared. I turned away to get to Greene Street side, but she disappeared. She disappeared from me. I went into the toilet rooms, I went out from the toilet rooms, bent my face over the sink, and then I went to the Washington Place side to the elevators but there was a big crowd. I saw a crowd around the door trying to open the door. There I saw Bernstein, the manager's brother, trying to open the door, but he couldn't. He left, and Margaret was there too, and she tried to open the door and she could not. I pushed her on the side and I tried to open the door, and I could not. And then she pushed me on the side and she said I will open the door, and she tried to open the door, and the big smoke came and Margaret Swartz I saw bending down on her knees. Her hair was loose and her dress was on the floor a little far from her. And then she screamed at the top of her voice open the door, fire, I am lost, My God I am lost, there is fire. And I went away from Margaret. I left and stood in the middle of the room, that is I went in in the dressing room first. There was a big crowd; I went out of the dressing room, went in the middle of the room between the machines and examining tables, and then I went in. I saw Bernstein, the manager's brother, going around the windows putting his head from the windows. He wanted to jump, I suppose, but he was afraid. He brought himself back and then I saw the flames cover him, and some other man on Greene Street, the flames covered him too. And then I turned my coat on the wrong side and put it on my head with the fur to my face, the lining on the outside, and then I got hold of a bunch of dresses and covered up the top of my head. I just got ready to go and somebody came and chased me back, pulled my dress back, and I kicked her with my foot and she disappeared. I tried to make my escape. I had a pocketbook on me and that pocketbook began to burn. I pressed it to my heart to extinguish the fire, and I made my escape right through the flames. The whole door was aflame right to the roof. It looked like a wall of flame? Like a red curtain of fire, she answers.

Question: Now there was something in that that you left out, I think, Miss Alperman. When Bernstein was jumping around do you remember what that was like? Like a wild cat, wasn't it? Answer: Like a wild cat. You left that out the second time. How long have you lived in Philadelphia? Then he comes back: You did leave that out, didn't you, just now when you told us about Bernstein, that he jumped around like a wild cat? Answer: Well, I don't imagine whether a wild cat or a wild dog. I just speak to imagine just exactly. How long have you lived in Philadelphia, he asks?

Page 1165: This is the third time, and he begins it by saying: Now, could you tell us again what you did after that time. And she says, after going out from the dressing room? And he says yes, and she goes on: I went to the Waverly side windows to look for fire escape. Margaret Swartz was with me and then Margaret disappeared. I called her to Greene Street. She disappeared and I went into the toilet room, went out, bent my face over the sink, and then I walked to the door to the Washington side to the elevator. I saw there a big crowd I couldn't push through. I saw around the Washington side door a whole lot of people standing. I pushed through there and I saw Bernstein, the manager's brother, trying to open the door. He could not, and he left. Margaret Swartz was there; she tried to open the door and she could not. I pushed Margaret on the side and I tried to open the door. I could not, and then Margaret pushed me on the other side and she tried to open the door. Big smoke came and Margaret bent on her knees, her trail was a little far from her just spreading on the floor far from her, and her hair was loose, and I saw the ends of her dress and the ends of her hair begin to burn. I went into the small dressing room; there was a big crowd and I tried, I stood there and I went out right away, pushed through and went out, and then I stood in the center of the room between the examining tables and the machines. There I noticed at Washington side windows Bernstein, the manager's brother, trying to jump from the window. He stuck his head out; he wanted to jump, but I suppose he was afraid. Then he would draw himself back, then I saw the flames cover him. He jumped like a wild cat on the walls, and then I stood, took my coat, covered my head, turning the fur to my head, the lining to the outside, got hold of a bunch of dresses that was lying on the tables and covered it up over my head, and I just wanted to go, and some lady came and she began to pull the back of my dress. I kicked her with my foot, I don't know where she got to, and then I had a purse with me and that purse began to burn. I pressed it to my heart to extinguish the fire. I ran through the fire, the whole door was aflame; it was a red curtain of fire. I went right on to the roof.

Page 1167: Question: (This is Steuer) What you told us here today, you didn't study that and tell it that way, did you? No, sir. You didn't study the words with which you were to tell it? No, sir. Do you remember that you got out to the center of the floor, do you remember that? I remember that I got out to the Greene Street door. You remember that you did get to the center of the floor, don't you? Question: Now tell us from there on what you did. Start at that point now, instead of at the beginning, that is the point being between the tables, between the machines and the examining table in the center. And she tells the fourth time now: In the beginning I saw Bernstein on the Washington side, Bernstein's brother going around like a wild cat. He wanted to jump out from the window, I suppose, but he was afraid, and then he brought himself back and the flames covered him, and I took my coat, turned it on the wrong side with the fur to my face and the lining on the outside, got hold of a bunch of dresses from the examining table, covered up my head, and I wanted to run, And then a lady came along and she began to pull my dress back; she wanted to pull me back, and I kicked her with my foot. I don't know where she got to, and I ran out through the Greene Street side door which was in flames; it was a red curtain of fire on that door, to the roof. Question: You never studied those words, did you? Answer: No, sir. Question: Now, Miss Alperman (This is by Bostwick), each time that you have answered Mr. Steuer's questions you have tried to repeat it in the same language that you first told it here in Court, have you not? Yes, sir. And you remember every detail of that story as well today as it happened yesterday? Yes, sir. And it is all true? All true, yes, sir. Steuer on re-cross: Can you tell that story in any other words than those you have told it in? Answer: In any other words? I remember it this way just exactly how it was done. Will you please answer my question; could you tell it in any other words? Probably I can. Then Bostwick: Will you state to the jury why you try to repeat the last time what you told Mr. Steuer in the same language that you used the first time you told Mr. Steuer. Answer: Because he asked me the very same story over and over; I tried to tell him the very same thing because he asked me the very same thing over and over. Question: And did you think you had to tell it in the same words? Answer: No, I didn't think, I just it the way he asked me to say it, over and over, and I told him in the same words.

Cornell University ILR School. Complete Transcript of Triangle Fire. http://law2.umkc.edu/faculty/projects/ftrials/lapd/kingvideo.html

Endnotes

1. Susan Saladoff, *Hot Coffee*, directed by Susan Saladoff (HBO 2011), DVD.

2. Scott Fraser, "The Problem With Eyewitness Testimony," May 2012. http://www.ted.com/talks/scott_fraser_the_problem_with_eyewitness_testimony?language=en.

3. American Experience. *Triangle Fire. (1996–2013)* http://www.pbs.org/wgbh/americanexperience/films/triangle/player/

4. Cornell University ILR School. Complete Transcript of Triangle Fire. http://digitalcommons.ilr.cornell.edu/triangletrans.

5. http://law2.umkc.edu/faculty/projects/ftrials/lapd/kingvideo.html

6. https://www.youtube.com/watch?v=puElaTZSakw

CHAPTER 2

Law, Economics, and Society

Chapter Learning Objectives

After completing this chapter, students should be able to:

- Discuss laws and legal concepts as they relate to the business environment.

- Explain a business organization's role in social responsibility.

- Describe the relationships that exist between businesses and their societal stakeholders.

- Consider responsibilities for ethical leadership that exist in contemporary organizations.

- Recognize the principles and practices of responsible corporate governance.

> "Let these truths be indelibly impressed on our minds—that we cannot be HAP-PY, without being FREE—that we cannot be free, without being secure in our property—that we cannot be secure in our property, if, without our consent, others may, as by right, take it away. . . ."
>
> —John Dickinson, *Letters from a Farmer in Pennsylvania XII* (1767, 1768)

Rules of the Game

A society is a community of people associated according to certain shared principles or interests. Members of a society relinquish some freedom of individual action in favor of society's purposes. For example, when members of a club agree to meet at a certain time, they have relinquished the right to be somewhere else at that time. When members of a nation pay taxes, they have relinquished the individual right to otherwise disposition those funds. Taxpayers expect the government to disposition the collected funds for society's benefit.

Government action for society's benefit, whether through the power to tax or through other regulatory power, limits individual freedom. The founders of the United States, who drafted the U.S. Constitution and the Bill of Rights, understood the concept of "property" broadly, to include not only real and personal property but also labor, and the fruits of labor in the form of wages. Control of one's property is a form of liberty. If the government can impose a tax or a fee on property without the consent of the governed, then the people are not secure;

if the people are not secure in their property then they are not free and without freedom there can be no happiness. (See quote from *Letters from a Farmer in Pennsylvania, above*).

The founders were keenly aware of the potential for conflict between individual freedoms and social benefit through government action. It was, after all, the unilateral levy of taxes and fees by the British government that drove the colonies to rebellion, even though the British government asserted the funds would be used for socially beneficial colonial military defense. A well-designed system of laws provides a mechanism for resolving the inevitable tensions between individual freedoms and social benefit without resorting to armed rebellion. The founders designed a social system in which widely distributed economic power, expressed through the democratic process, serves as a limitation on central government overreach through an integration of democracy and capitalism.

democracy

government by the people directly or through elected representatives

They were also well acquainted with the principles of capitalism and the economic theories of Adam Smith. In 1759, Adam Smith used the metaphor of an "invisible hand" to describe how market participants, each acting in his own self-interest, optimize resource utilization and maximize their own wealth. In so doing, competitive free market forces, unencumbered by government over-regulation, drive out waste, encourage innovation, and maintain pricing equilibrium. The result is greater prosperity for all.

capitalism

an economic system in which the means of production are privately owned goods and services which are produced for profit

We continue to debate the proper balance of government oversight and individual freedom. All business enterprises must deal with some amount of regulation. Deregulation evangelists argue that free market discipline and otherwise efficient market forces have been undermined by government intervention and regulation. Advocates of regulation argue that regulation may be necessary generally in two broad categories: (1) to protect the "little guy" in an asymmetrical economic transaction; or (2) to preserve a public resource. Whatever the issue may be—product safety, banking disclosures, air quality, sick leave, motor vehicle operation, day care, tax collection—the perpetual questions are: Is government too powerful? Is business too burdened? Are the people, individually and collectively, protected from intrusive government and from rapacious business practices?

In this chapter, you will consider some recent examples of free market principles applied to market segments in which a government entity traditionally provides some or all of the goods and services. You will choose one of the three market segments described below and write a short essay (approximately 1,000 words) discussing the application of free market principles to that market segment. You will present and defend your position to the class in an oral summary.

In your essay you will:

1. Explain <u>in your own words</u> Adam Smith's theory of free markets and the meaning of the invisible hand metaphor;

2. Describe the market segment you have chosen to write about;

3. Analyze whether or not, and to what extent, the mechanics of a free market, such as willing buyer-willing seller, elasticity, and uniform access to information, operate in that market segment;

4. State your conclusion, supported by your arguments, as to whether or not, and to what extent, the market segment you have chosen to write about should be governed by free market discipline or regulated by the government.

CHAPTER ORGANIZATION

Health Care: Market Medicine

Prisons for Profit

Schools for Sale

Health Care: Market Medicine

Health care in the United States is generally recognized as being expensive and inefficient when compared to the health care systems of comparable industrial nations. Political conservatives argue that free market solutions offer the best tools to address the issues. Progressives argue that health care is a social good that cannot be left to the rough justice of the free market. In a free market, a fair price is the price at which goods or services change hands between a willing buyer and a willing seller, neither being under any compulsion to buy or to sell and both having reasonable knowledge of relevant facts. Does this description apply to health care? In a free market, sellers are incentivized to reduce costs in order to increase profits; shouldn't we reduce costs by eliminating wasteful processes? Should we refuse treatment for people who cannot pay? If your answer is no, then who should pay for them? If the management of a for-profit hospital has a fiduciary duty to shareholders to maximize profits, then how should the for-profit hospital deal with patients who cannot pay? What about drug and medical device manufacturers? Home care providers? Other?

Prisons for Profit

Why do we put people in prison? The classic answer is to punish the wrongdoer, to rehabilitate the wrongdoer and to protect the public. All societies must grapple with the purpose and effectiveness of imprisonment and the issues are universal: How do we define rehabilitation? How do we measure the benefit to society of locking up a dangerous person for twenty or forty or sixty years? How do we integrate law enforcement, criminal justice, and the penal system so that goals and investments are aligned?

Since the 1990s, for-profit prisons have flourished in the United States. Two for-profit prison companies, GEO and Corrections Corporation of America (CCA), earn combined $3.3 billion in annual revenue. The private federal prison population doubled from 2000 to 2010.[1] Government officials are stewards of the public purse. They are duty-bound to administer their responsibilities cost-effectively. For-profit prison management companies promise to lower the cost of prison operations, and they bind themselves by contract to deliver on that promise.

That same contract also compels the government agency—local, state, or federal—to maintain a certain occupancy rate, and to pay a penalty if occupancy rates fall. This provision is not unusual in certain types of long-term commercial contracts. The contractor is committing resources for an extended period and some protection for its profit margins is reasonable. The management of a for-profit prison has a fiduciary duty to shareholders to maximize profits.

Is it appropriate for a for-profit prison company to seek to influence social policy in support of its occupancy rates? For-profit prison companies and their lobbyists authored many of the three strikes statutes and legislative changes to mandatory minimums, both of which resulted in higher incarceration rates. The following is an excerpt from CCA's 2014 annual report:

> The demand for our facilities and services could be adversely affected by the relaxation of enforcement efforts, leniency in conviction or parole standards and sentencing practices or through the decriminalization of certain activities that are currently proscribed by our criminal laws. For instance, any changes with respect to drugs and controlled substances or illegal immigration could

affect the number of persons arrested, convicted, and sentenced, thereby potentially reducing demand for correctional facilities to house them. . . . Legislation has been proposed in numerous jurisdictions that could lower minimum sentences for some non-violent crimes and make more inmates eligible for early release based on good behavior.[2]

Have we forfeited our social responsibility by contracting prison operations to for-profit entities, or is this a wise cost-control measure?

Schools for Sale

A functioning democracy requires an educated electorate. Public schools provide free K–12 education throughout the United States, paid for with tax revenues. Before the 1960s, funding and control of public schools was exclusively local. In the 1960s, federal funds were allocated to local schools and federal oversight followed. Concerns about test scores and student performance in a globalized economy drove initiatives to innovate and improve, such as the programs known as No Child Left Behind and Common Core. Those initiatives included experimentation with for-profit public schools.

For-profit school management proposals promise cost-reductions through market-driven efficiencies. Inherent in these proposals is the principle that private, for-profit companies can always operate an enterprise more efficiently than a government entity. One lawmaker in Mississippi favorably compared for-profit schools to for-profit prison operations, noting that in his state the for-profit prison operators are required to run the prisons for 10 percent less than the government's operating cost.[3] It is a truism that public schools are not awash in extra funds. What cost reductions will the for-profit school management companies make in order to be more efficient and have enough money left over to pay dividends to its shareholders? Does the payment of dividends supersede teacher bonuses? Is it appropriate to channel local tax revenue collected for local school operations to private investors, the shareholders of the for-profit company, whoever and wherever they may be? Do the answers to these questions depend upon whether or not the for-profit company can deliver improved academic performance?

Endnotes

1. Cohen, Michael. "How for-profit prisons have become the biggest lobby no one is talking about." http://www.washingtonpost.com/posteverything/wp/2015/04/28/how-for-profit-prisons-have-become-the-biggest-lobby-no-one-is-talking-about/

2. Id.

3. Carr, Sarah and Gilbertson, Annie. "New skepticism of for-profit companies managing public schools." http://hechingerreport.org/new-skepticism-of-for-profit-companies-managing-public-schools/

CHAPTER 3

Law, Ethics, and Decision Making

Chapter Learning Objectives

After completing this chapter, students should be able to:

- Define ethics and evaluate business strategies based on ethical principles.

- Explain a business organization's role in social responsibility.

- Recognize the social and ethical issues facing business organizations in today's environment and the implications of managerial decisions that are made in response to them.

- Describe the relationships that exist between businesses and their societal stakeholders.

- Consider responsibilities for ethical leadership that exist in contemporary organizations.

- Recognize the principles and practices of responsible corporate governance.

> Alice: Would you tell me, please, which way I ought to go from here?
>
> The Cheshire Cat: That depends a good deal on where you want to get to.
>
> Alice: I don't much care where.
>
> The Cheshire Cat: Then it doesn't much matter which way you go.
>
> —*Alice in Wonderland*, Lewis Carroll (1865)

Rules of the Game

The study of business law and ethics, like any other subject, can be pursued in a textbook or in a classroom. But it's not in the classroom, it's in the boardroom, where the learning really matters. How well do you think you will perform when your decisions affect the real lives of real people? When real money will be gained or lost because of your decisions? In this chapter, you will participate in a simulation designed to replicate the real world. To the substantive content of your learning, the simulation will add conflict, competition, and the clock. Welcome to the Board of Directors of Smartfence, Inc.

The Smartfence simulation is a team project in which students role-play entrepreneurs founding and launching a tech startup called "Smartfence." Teams consist of either four or five students, each of whom is assigned a particular role. Teams and roles are assigned for the duration of the simulation. The four-person team roles are CEO, CFO, VP Marketing, and VP Operations. The five-person teams add VP Human Resources to the original four. Handouts specific to each role summarize the respective characters' backstories, including risk tolerance, long-term goals, and technical strengths and weaknesses. Students assume the characteristics ascribed to their respective roles and remain in character during each simulation session.

Each character is a founder and executive of the new company. All attend the Board of Directors (BoD) meetings. The BoD meets four times to address specific issues such as health and safety problems, contract disputes, and compliance matters. During the BoD meetings each student, *in character*, will advocate for an outcome that reflects his or her character-specific attributes. In subsequent sessions, more information is distributed which builds on the previous session's work and presents new issues.

Each session begins with distribution of Background and Character Facts. All participants read the Background, which explains the reason for the BoD meeting. The team has a fixed amount of time, usually sixty to ninety minutes to address the issues identified in the Background. In addition to the Background, each student reviews the Character Facts specific to that student's role. For example, each team has a CEO and all the CEOs receive the same Character Facts, which are of course different from the Character Facts pertaining to the other roles. During the meeting, each student will advocate for an outcome *in the character of the assigned role*, reflecting the character-specific attributes and positions identified in the Character Facts.

Also, from time to time Additional Facts may arise which require real-time adjustments to strategies and conclusions. During the meeting, the BoD identifies the issues, makes decisions taking into account the information in the various fact distributions, and records the decisions, including appropriate explanations, in draft BoD Minutes. The BoD approves the draft BoD Minutes and submits them at the end of the session.

Each team submits an *informal draft or outline* of BoD meeting Minutes which records in summary or outline form the major decisions taken by the Board and the reasoning behind those decisions. In Session 1, each team selects a scribe who is responsible for the Minutes for all four sessions as follows: (i) recording the Minutes during the meetings, (ii) obtaining BoD member initials indicating concurrence; and (iii) submitting the Minutes by e-mail or by flash drive before the class is dismissed at the end of the session.

CHAPTER ORGANIZATION

Session 1: The Founders

    4-member team

    5-member team

Session 2: The Investigation

    4-member team

    5-member team

Session 3: Goodbye Yellow Brick Road

    4-member team

    5-member team

Session 4: How Do You Sleep at Night?

    4-member team

    5-member team

Session 1: The Founders—4-member team

BACKGROUND

A group of entrepreneurs (the "Founders") has come together to launch a venture. Each of them has a particular skill set: finance, engineering, operations, and marketing. The engineer, whose name is Mr. Wizard and the marketing specialist, Ms. Winfrey, collaborated on development of a new security product called the "Smartfence." The Smartfence is a security system that incorporates proprietary software and proprietary sensor design to detect, analyze, and identify intruders. The competitive advantage of the Smartfence system is the speed and reliability of threat detection and identification. They have built and tested a prototype system and are ready to bring the product to market.

At the launch of any new venture, the principals are swept along on a wave of enthusiasm and hope. Soon enough, reality intrudes in the form of market issues, customer requirements, technical problems, financing, and all the many challenges they must overcome. As they travel the entrepreneurial road together, they may find their challenges compounded if, at the time the venture is launched, they don't adequately address the issues associated with <u>formation</u>, <u>investment</u>, <u>control</u>, and <u>exit strategies</u>. The Founders of Smartfence are aware of these issues, and wish to structure their new venture appropriately so that the risks created by these issues are mitigated as much as possible. They are meeting today to reach agreement on these issues, and to execute a Memorandum of Understanding documenting their decisions.

Each of the Founders will be an <u>active</u> participant in Smartfence, and will work full-time for the company. Mr. Wizard, who is primarily responsible for the technical concepts, will have technical responsibility for effective transition from prototype to volume production. Ms. Winfrey will be responsible for marketing, advertising, and sales. Mr. Goodwrench, who will manage the company's Operations department, is somewhat older than his colleagues, and he brings many years of experience in volume production, including supplier management and quality control. Mr. Moneypenny's credentials include a BA in Accounting and an MBA from Wharton, and he is a CPA. He will have the position of Chief Financial Officer.

The Founders need $500,000.00 in cash to begin operations. Mr. Wizard will contribute the proprietary software and sensor design, which is valued at $250,000.00. Ms. Winfrey, widely recognized as a marketing genius, has already done the initial strategic planning for introducing the Smartfence to the market, and the intellectual property resulting from her work to date (the strategic, marketing, and sales plans) is valued at $100,000.00. Mr. Goodwrench is prepared to invest up to $250,000.00 in the venture. Mr. Moneypenny is also prepared to invest, and has up to $500,000.00 available for that purpose.

The Founders have incorporated their venture as "Smartfence, Inc." under the laws of the State of Florida, and the corporation has authorized 10,000 shares of Class A Common stock and 10,000 shares of Class B Preferred stock. They know that stock ownership encompasses economic participation (positive and negative) and the right to some level of participation in decision making for the company.

The Founders are meeting today to identify and agree on the basic principles which will define and govern your relationships going forward. The decisions reached today will subsequently be formalized in a Memorandum of Understanding by your counsel. For today, you will document your points of agreement in summary form. Each participant will attest to agreement by initialing the written summary. At a minimum, your summary must address the following:

1. Each of the Founders will contribute a skill or ability, or something of value to the venture. How much stock and of what class should each receive and why?

2. How will decision-making authority be allocated? Who will be on the Board of Directors? Should there be a different standard of participation for major events such as bankruptcy, dissolution, sale of all the assets, a merger, or a major acquisition? What if the Board votes 50–50? Who will be the President of the company and why?

3. What responsibilities will each Founder have for capital calls if more cash is needed?

4. What will happen to a Founder's stock if the person leaves the company? May the company buy it back? Must the company buy it back? Will the stock price be valued at fair market value, or by some other method? May he take the stock with him? If yes, does his successor also become an owner, receiving stock, which dilutes the remaining shares?

5. Should there be any restrictions on stock transfer to third parties? What if one of the Founders wants to sell? What if one of the Founders dies? How long should these restrictions be in force?

6. What about the proprietary information? Who owns it? Are there to be any constraints on Mr. Wizard if he leaves the company? What about Ms. Winfrey?

7. Initially all of the Founders will be full-time employees of the company. Under what circumstances can one of the Founders be terminated, and what are the consequences to that person's stock ownership?

CHARACTER FACTS

Mr. Goodwrench

What you specifically want is to successfully launch the company—but with an exit strategy for you. You see the promise in this venture and you are willing to invest your cash and your talent to get it started. However, you have other plans, and intend to retire from Smartfence after five years <u>at the latest.</u> You are counting on the return on your investment after you retire, and will not accept any stock arrangements that unduly jeopardize those returns. Because of your experience, you are well qualified to run the company and get it started.

Mr. Moneypenny

You are the CFO, you are good at your job and you know how unforeseen events can disrupt business associations. You would like to ride this venture to the top, and be a major contributor to its growth and expansion along the way. You are particularly concerned about the provisions in the MOU, which address what happens to a Founder's stock if that person quits or is fired. You are also concerned about what might happen if Mr. Wizard leaves the company for some reason, and you think that Mr. Wizard should be subject to a noncompete if he leaves. You are concerned about the potential for a deadlock on the Board of Directors, and will insist that there be an odd number of directors or some other mechanism to break a tie, even if that means bringing in an outside director.

Ms. Winfrey

You are a business development and marketing whiz-kid with a hot degree (a Sloan MBA) and no money. You turned down some high-profile job offers when you graduated from Sloan to get in on the ground floor at Smartfence. You invested your time and talent to create a plan that will get the product to market in record time. You need to see steady cash flow soon, to pay off your student loans. Your career prospects are wide open. You are willing to work for less money now in exchange for future high-profit incentives.

Mr. Wizard

You are willing to turn over complete ownership of your software and sensor design to the company, although you feel that the $250,000.00 valuation is a little low. You believe that the product will be very successful, so you are willing to accept this low valuation now in exchange for an expected high return in the profits the company makes from sale of the product. You picture yourself in Silicon Valley, sometime in the future, at a black-tie charity auction dinner sitting next to Steve Jobs. You want immediate and high dividend distributions on your shares. How the company is run on a day-to-day basis is boring to you, but you pay attention because you want to make sure money is there when it's time for you to cash out.

Session 1: The Founders—5-member team

BACKGROUND

A group of entrepreneurs (the "Founders") has come together to launch a venture. Each of them has a particular skill set: finance, engineering, operations, marketing, and HR. The engineer, whose name is Mr. Wizard and the marketing specialist, Ms. Winfrey, collaborated on development of a new security product called the "Smartfence." The Smartfence is a security system which incorporates proprietary software and proprietary sensor design to detect, analyze, and identify intruders. The competitive advantage of the Smartfence system is the speed and reliability of threat detection and identification. They have built and tested a prototype system and are ready to bring the product to market.

At the launch of any new venture, the principals are swept along on a wave of enthusiasm and hope. Soon enough, reality intrudes in the form of market issues, customer requirements, technical problems, financing, and all the many challenges they must overcome. As they travel the entrepreneurial road together, they may find their challenges compounded if, at the time the venture is launched, they don't adequately address the issues associated with formation, investment, control, and exit strategies. The Founders of Smartfence are aware of these issues, and wish to structure their new venture appropriately so that the risks created by these issues are mitigated as much as possible. They are meeting today to reach agreement on these issues, and to execute a Memorandum of Understanding documenting their decisions.

Each of the Founders will be an active participant in Smartfence, and will work full-time for the company. Mr. Wizard, who is primarily responsible for the technical concepts, will have technical responsibility for effective transition from prototype to volume production. Ms. Winfrey will be responsible for marketing, advertising, and sales. Mr. Goodwrench, who will manage the company's Operations department, is somewhat older than his colleagues, and he brings many years of experience in volume production, including supplier management and quality control. Mr. Moneypenny's credentials include a BA in Accounting and an MBA from Wharton, and he is a CPA. He will have the position of Chief Financial Officer. Mr. Donaghy is an experienced professional in the field of Human Resources (although he sometimes overvalues his abilities) and he will be the head of HR.

The Founders need $500,000.00 in cash to begin operations. Mr. Wizard will contribute the proprietary software and sensor design, which is valued at $250,000.00. Ms. Winfrey, widely recognized as a marketing genius, has already done the initial strategic planning for introducing the Smartfence to the market, and the intellectual property resulting from her work to date (the strategic, marketing, and sales plans) is valued at $100,000.00. Mr. Goodwrench is prepared to invest up to $250,000.00 in the venture. Mr. Moneypenny is also prepared to invest, and has up to $500,000.00 available for that purpose. Mr. Donaghy is reluctant to invest, but has accumulated savings of $100,000.00.

The Founders have incorporated their venture as "Smartfence, Inc." under the laws of the State of Florida, and the corporation has authorized 10,000 shares of Class A Common stock and 10,000 shares of Class B Preferred stock. They know that stock ownership encompasses economic participation (positive and negative) and the right to some level of participation in decision making for the company.

The Founders are meeting today to identify and agree on the basic principles which will define and govern your relationships going forward. The decisions reached today will subsequently be formalized in a Memorandum of Understanding by your counsel. For today, you will document your points of agreement in summary form. Each participant will attest to agreement by initialing the written summary. At a minimum, your summary must address the following:

1. Each of the Founders will contribute a skill or ability, or something of value to the venture. How much stock and of what class should each receive and why?

2. How will decision-making authority be allocated? Who will be on the Board of Directors? Should there be a different standard of participation for major events such as bankruptcy, dissolution, sale

of all the assets, a merger, or a major acquisition? What if the Board votes 50–50? Who will be the President of the company and why?

3. What responsibilities will each Founder have for capital calls if more cash is needed?

4. What will happen to a Founder's stock if the person leaves the company? May the company buy it back? Must the company buy it back? Will the stock price be valued at fair market value, or by some other method? May he take the stock with him? If yes, does his successor also become an owner, receiving stock, which dilutes the remaining shares?

5. Should there be any restrictions on stock transfer to third parties? What if one of the Founders wants to sell? What if one of the Founders dies? How long should these restrictions be in force?

6. What about the proprietary information? Who owns it? Are there to be any constraints on Mr. Wizard if he leaves the company? What about Ms. Winfrey?

7. Initially all of the Founders will be full-time employees of the company. Under what circumstances can one of the Founders be terminated, and what are the consequences to that person's stock ownership?

CHARACTER FACTS

Mr. Donaghy

You are the head of HR and you're good at your job when you pay attention to it. You are very conservative and risk-averse. Your first answer to everything is always "No." You are interested in job security and a paycheck. You think the most stable structure for the venture would be one which makes it difficult to change the structure and difficult to leave the organization. You are concerned about what might happen if Mr. Wizard leaves the company for some reason and you think that Wizard should be subject to a rigorous, unbreakable noncompete should he leave. You do not want any outsiders on the Board of Directors.

Mr. Goodwrench

What you specifically want is to successfully launch the company—but with an exit strategy for you. You see the promise in this venture and you are willing to invest your cash and your talent to get it started. However, you have other plans, and intend to retire from Smartfence after five years at the latest. You are counting on the return on your investment after you retire, and will not accept any stock arrangements which unduly jeopardize those returns. Because of your experience, you are well-qualified to run the company and get it started.

Mr. Moneypenny

You are the CFO, you are good at your job and you know how unforeseen events can disrupt business associations. You would like to ride this venture to the top, and be a major contributor to its growth and expansion along the way. You are particularly concerned about the provisions in the MOU which address what happens to a Founder's stock if that person quits or is fired. You are also concerned about what might happen if Mr. Wizard leaves the company for some reason, and you think that Mr. Wizard should be subject to a noncompete if he leaves. You are concerned about the potential for a deadlock on the Board of Directors, and will insist that there be an odd number of directors or some other mechanism to break a tie, even if that means bringing in an outside director.

Ms. Winfrey

You are a business development and marketing whiz-kid with a hot degree (a Sloan MBA) and no money. You turned down some high-profile job offers when you graduated from Sloan to get in on the ground floor at Smartfence. You invested your time and talent to create a plan that will get the product to market in record time. You need to see steady cash flow soon, to pay off your student loans. Your career prospects are wide open. You are willing to work for less money now in exchange for future high-profit incentives.

Mr. Wizard

You are willing to turn over complete ownership of your software and sensor design to the company, although you feel that the $250,000.00 valuation is a little low. You believe that the product will be very successful, so you are willing to accept this low valuation now in exchange for an expected high return in the profits the company makes from sale of the product. You picture yourself in Silicon Valley, sometime in the future, at a black-tie charity auction dinner sitting next to Bill Gates. You want immediate and high dividend distributions on your shares. How the company is run on a day-to-day basis is boring to you, but you pay attention because you want to make sure money is there when it's time for you to cash out.

Session 2: The Investigation—4-member team

BACKGROUND

The founders have agreed on the broad outline of their operating relationships and are prepared to move forward with their company. All the founders are members of the Board, with one vote each. You have unanimously agreed that Mr. Goodwrench will serve as President of the company.

Through a rigorous analytical process led by Mr. Goodwrench, you approved a business plan that will guide your actions for the next twelve months. You decided to invest in an unexpected government contract opportunity for a production contract, which you competitively bid for and won. Smartfence is now a government contractor with the Department of Homeland Security. You found a suitable production facility but did not have enough money to purchase or rent it. You were able to negotiate a joint venture with the facility's owner, Bigoil; according to the joint venture agreement Smartfence operates the production facility and Bigoil has accepted 2,000 shares of preferred stock and will receive preferred dividends in lieu of rent. You have launched full-scale production on the government contract and on some smaller commercial contracts and you have 150 employees on the production line. The government contract is providing a strong revenue stream and your sales revenues are higher than anticipated.

The government contract schedule is very tight and the margins are small. If Smartfence misses any deliveries at all on the government contract, Homeland Security will declare the contract in breach and send the business to the next higher bidder. If that occurs, Smartfence will be liable for the difference between the new vendor's price and its own contract price to the government ("excess cost of reprocurement"). If that were to happen, all anticipated excess cash flow would be consumed in reprocurement costs, and there would be no money to pay any dividends, preferred or common.

The company is running two production lines simultaneously in order to meet the government contract schedule requirements. One of the manufacturing steps involves immersing the fencing material into a tank containing a chemical bath. The chemical bath is toxic and hazardous. Both of the tanks (one on each production line) were built by a reputable manufacturer. The tanks are concrete, lined with an impermeable material, and built carefully to strict specifications. Each of the tanks was inspected and installed by experts, and is brand-new. The company is three weeks into production. <u>Thirty minutes ago</u> one of the tank liners cracked, the chemical bath spilled onto the manufacturing floor, some of the chemical bath overflowed into drains in the floor which lead to stormwater drains, and several employees who voluntarily engaged in emergency cleanup are reporting having difficulty breathing, which they attribute to having inhaled chemical fumes.

All production on the damaged line has halted. The Board has convened an emergency meeting to decide what to do.

Identify the issues you're facing and record your decisions concerning how to deal with those issues. Your answer should include <u>communications</u> and <u>strategy recommendations</u> with respect to:

- The tank manufacturer
- The joint venture partner/property owner

- The possibly injured employees
- Government customer (Homeland Security)
- Commercial customers
- Other stakeholders? *(at least two "others")*

CHARACTER FACTS

Mr. Goodwrench

You have already heard from Bigoil's CEO and General Counsel, and their Director of Environmental Services is on the way over to the plant. (How did they find out?) They have already made it clear that they expect to be given total access to Smartfence's books and records, including management memos concerning the selection of the tank vendor as well as all quality records. You are also thinking about the government contract, and wondering if perhaps you could complete the government contract on the other production line, and postpone or renegotiate the non-government contracts. You have ordered all employees (excluding the injured and those engaged in emergency response) to assemble in the cafeteria.

Mr. Moneypenny

You are in full crisis management mode. You have already called the company's general counsel, who is on the way over. You have alerted your direct reports with instructions to plan for a 24/7 effort until the spill is dealt with and production resumed, if it ever is resumed. You are extremely annoyed with what appears to be naiveté on the part of your associates, especially Goodwrench; they don't seem to realize how terribly serious this environmental spill really is. You are not interested in going to jail for an environmental crime, and you know the regulators will be looking for a scapegoat. You argue firmly that the company must immediately draft a statement, taking into account all the different stakeholders who will hear the statement. The statement must reassure the workforce, the shareholders, the customers, and the public that appropriate steps are being taken to remedy the situation, and assert unequivocally that the company will return to full production <u>as soon as it is safe to do so and not a moment before.</u>

Ms. Winfrey

You recognize the impact of this catastrophe immediately. The government contract will probably be terminated for default, and Smartfence will have to pay the excess costs of reprocurement, thereby guaranteeing no dividends. You won't let the door hit you on the way out, but you have to plan your exit strategy and try to get a good severance package. You're thinking maybe you can leverage a couple of off-color remarks Mr. Goodwrench made into a sexual harassment claim, and then they'll give you a fat severance package to go away. Your best bet is to stretch things out for a little bit until you can solidify your strategy, so you're supporting the investigation proposal.

Mr. Wizard

You are furious and frightened. You blame the vendor of the tank, and argue that Smartfence ought to demand that the manufacturer provide a replacement tank immediately. Because of your technical expertise, you volunteer to lead a team to investigate the cause of the failure.

Instructors: See Chapter 6 for additional facts which will introduce unexpected issues requiring urgent attention. These new issues can be introduced from time to time at your discretion.

Session 2: The Investigation—5-member team

BACKGROUND

The founders have agreed on the broad outline of their operating relationships and are prepared to move forward with their company. All the founders are members of the Board, with one vote each. You have unanimously agreed that Mr. Goodwrench will serve as President of the company.

Through a rigorous analytical process led by Mr. Goodwrench, you approved a business plan that will guide your actions for the next twelve months. You decided to invest in an unexpected government contract opportunity for a production contract, which you competitively bid for and won. Smartfence is now a government contractor with the Department of Homeland Security. You found a suitable production facility but did not have enough money to purchase or rent it. You were able to negotiate a joint venture with the facility's owner, Bigoil; according to the joint venture agreement Smartfence operates the production facility and Bigoil has accepted 2,000 shares of preferred stock and will receive preferred dividends in lieu of rent. You have launched full-scale production on the government contract and on some smaller commercial contracts and you have 150 employees on the production line. The government contract is providing a strong revenue stream and your sales revenues are higher than anticipated.

The government contract schedule is very tight and the margins are small. If Smartfence misses any deliveries at all on the government contract, Homeland Security will declare the contract in breach and send the business to the next higher bidder. If that occurs, Smartfence will be liable for the difference between the new vendor's price and its own contract price to the government ("excess cost of reprocurement"). If that were to happen, all anticipated excess cash flow would be consumed in reprocurement costs, and there would be no money to pay any dividends, preferred or common.

The company is running two production lines simultaneously in order to meet the government contract schedule requirements. One of the manufacturing steps involves immersing the fencing material into a tank containing a chemical bath. The chemical bath is toxic and hazardous. Both of the tanks (one on each production line) were built by a reputable manufacturer. The tanks are concrete, lined with an impermeable material, and built carefully to strict specifications. Each of the tanks was inspected and installed by experts, and is brand-new. The company is three weeks into production. Thirty minutes ago one of the tank liners cracked, the chemical bath spilled onto the manufacturing floor, some of the chemical bath overflowed into drains in the floor which lead to stormwater drains, and several employees who voluntarily engaged in emergency cleanup are reporting having difficulty breathing, which they attribute to having inhaled chemical fumes.

All production on the damaged line has halted. The Board has convened an emergency meeting to decide what to do.

Identify the issues you're facing and record your decisions concerning how to deal with those issues. Your answer should include communications and strategy recommendations with respect to:

- The tank manufacturer
- The joint venture partner/property owner
- The possibly injured employees
- Government customer (Homeland Security)
- Commercial customers
- Other stakeholders? (at least two "others")

CHARACTER FACTS

Mr. Donaghy

You are fully capable of dealing with this issue, and you know how important it is to behave professionally and calmly. You suspect that Ms. Winfrey has never faced this sort of problem before, based on her behavior and her comments; she appears to believe this is a catastrophe on the order of Noah's flood, which it certainly is not. Moneypenny's hysteria isn't helping either. Thanks to you, the company has a robust training and safety program, and keeps meticulous records of its compliance. You argue firmly that the company must immediately draft a statement, taking into account all the different stakeholders who will hear the statement. The statement must reassure the workforce, the shareholders, the customers, and the public that appropriate steps are being taken to remedy the situation, and assert unequivocally that the company will return to full production as soon as it is safe to do so and not a moment before. You have seen this sort of thing before, and think all the uproar is a bit immature.

Mr. Goodwrench

You have already heard from Bigoil's CEO and General Counsel, and their Director of Environmental Services is on the way over to the plant. (How did they find out?) They have already made it clear that they expect to be given total access to Smartfence's books and records, including management memos concerning the selection of the tank vendor as well as all quality records. Mr. Goodwrench also is thinking about the government contract, and wondering if perhaps you could complete the government contract on the other production line, and postpone or renegotiate the non-government contracts. You have ordered all employees (excluding the injured and those engaged in emergency response) to assemble in the cafeteria.

Mr. Moneypenny

You are in full crisis management mode. You have already called the company's general counsel, who is on the way over. You have alerted your direct reports with instructions to plan for a 24/7 effort until the spill is dealt with and production resumed, if it ever is resumed. You are extremely annoyed with what appears to be naiveté on the part of your associates, especially Goodwrench; they don't seem to realize how terribly serious this environmental spill really is. You are not interested in going to jail for an environmental crime, and you know the regulators will be looking for a scapegoat.

Ms. Winfrey

You recognize the impact of this catastrophe immediately. The government contract will probably be terminated for default, and Smartfence will have to pay the excess costs of reprocurement, thereby guaranteeing no dividends. You won't let the door hit you on the way out, but you have to plan your exit strategy and try to get a good severance package. You're thinking maybe you can leverage a couple of off-color remarks Mr. Goodwrench made into a sexual harassment claim, and then they'll give you a fat severance package to go away. Your best bet is to stretch things out for a little bit until you can solidify your strategy, so you're supporting the investigation proposal.

Mr. Wizard

You are furious and frightened. You blame the vendor of the tank, and argue that Smartfence ought to demand that the manufacturer provide a replacement tank immediately. Because of your technical expertise, you volunteer to lead a team to investigate the cause of the failure.

Instructors: See Chapter 6 for additional facts which will introduce unexpected issues requiring urgent attention. These new issues can be introduced from time to time at your discretion.

Session 3: Goodbye Yellow Brick Road—4-member team

Background

Smartfence survived the toxic spill, thanks to the supplier, who stepped up and provided interim facilities while the defect was repaired. Six months later, the company projects $15 million in sales, with the possibility of franchising and outsourcing. The company now has 100 employees. Walmart is interested in a modified product that could be sold to households, and suggests the possibility of selling 10,000 units annually, but requires a 60 percent reduction in price the first year and a 5 percent price reduction each of the succeeding three years.

The Company is targeting an IPO (initial public offering) in nine to twelve months. If the IPO is successful, Mr. Wizard may be able to depart with his cash, and buy that home on the ridge in Los Gatos. Mr. Goodwrench may be able to retire earlier than he had hoped. Ms. Winfrey, who dropped her secret plan to pursue a severance package (did she tell everyone about that?), sees big dollar signs as she rides the wave to global prominence. Mr. Moneypenny dreams of empire—legions of accountants and financial analysts, all reporting to him. All depends upon a successful IPO.

The Board reviewed advice from a prominent consultant:

The Company has reached that point in the growth of a business in which you need to bring in the "I have done this before" managers. This is not the time to reinvent the wheel because the failure to execute crisply in the next year could very likely result in the loss of business partners and customers, and make an IPO all but impossible. As this Company moves from a "few Chiefs, many Indians" structure to a layered management structure, it will undergo some severe organizational stress. Bringing in the second generation of management may require you to tell the loyal, hard-working, early-stage people that their career tracks are limited or have to be redirected. It is tough to do this to someone who took early-stage risk, did all-nighters for long stretches of time, did whatever had to be done to make the enterprise successful. This is why you have to make sure that the early stagers have an adequate stock position in the company. Speaking of stock, how will you attract the quality second-generation management types? The Securities and Exchange Commission looks very carefully at stock and option grants in the 12 months before the IPO. If the price of these grants does not ramp up toward the expected IPO price, the SEC may make the company re-price the stock grants and take charges to earnings, which can kill an IPO. This ramp up requirement will limit this Company's ability to use "cheap stock" to attract good people. With the lag time to find and recruit quality managers, it will most likely be a minimum of three to six months before most of them can be on the job. There won't be much time to integrate them into the business, continue to grow the business, and still hit a 9 to 12 month IPO target.

As the Company gets closer to the IPO the senior management team, which has been the driving force behind the Company's growth and which has the contacts with the strategic partners, will be diverted into financing issues and IPO. This will leave a management gap at just the time when extra attention will be required to manage the assimilation of the new people and channel the resulting "culture shift." Hey nobody said this stuff was easy.[1]

The Board members understand that it is time to review the current and future staffing needs, and to create a "now" and "later" organization chart for their areas of responsibility. Each of the founders must define the strategic needs of his or her area and discuss the backgrounds and skill sets of the current team as they related to meeting these needs.

Record what emerges from your strategies and skills review, taking into account:

1.   The Founders are talented, hard-working, and loyal; after all they have grown the business to $15M. But are the Founders capable of taking the Company to the next level? What qualifications and skills do they need to manage an IPO?

2. If the Founders divert their focus to the IPO, who will run the Company for the next nine months during the IPO?

3. Assuming the IPO is successful, will the Founders be capable of managing the Company after it goes public? What qualifications and skills will they need to manage a publicly-traded company?

4. Assuming one or more of the Founders will not survive the IPO because they can't (or won't) step up to new responsibilities, how should they be incentivized to leave?

5. How will the post-IPO second generation managers be compensated?

6 and 7. Other issues that may emerge during the Board meeting.

CHARACTER FACTS

Mr. Goodwrench

You are keen to supervise the handover to the second-generation team but not prepared to relinquish your position for another three years. You are excited about the prospect of learning new manufacturing techniques and the opportunity to start new manufacturing operations overseas. You're insistent that expansion must be led by experienced investment bankers and marketing professionals even though they must be paid more than Ms. Winfrey. You argue that too much is at stake to risk it all on an untested marketing guru, no matter how brilliant she may be. You think the talk of franchising is silly and distracting from the IPO, and don't want to spend any time on it.

Mr. Moneypenny

You plan to be the CFO of Smartfence until you drop dead at your desk many, many years from now. You think all marketing people are overpaid anyway (they don't really do anything except hire consultants to make pretty PowerPoint presentations with full color graphics) and you are willing to retain Ms. Winfrey and leave her in charge of marketing because she is paid less than more experienced marketing professionals. You are absolutely convinced that franchising is the way to go for two reasons: first, less capital is required, and second, following from the first point, less capital will be needed in the IPO—leaving more control in the Founders' hands. You acknowledge that vertical integration, including outsourcing to foreign manufacturing, would generate higher returns but point out that the risk is proportionately greater.

Ms. Winfrey

You are in this for the long haul. You see the opportunity for exponential growth, and have no intention of relinquishing your position as marketing goddess. You recognize the need for additional skills at the executive level with respect to the other Founders, but believe your own recent education at a top-flight business school is appropriately current for what is required. You think Mr. Goodwrench is an old fuddy-duddy who will stand in the way of implementing the cost-reduction methods you must embrace to meet Walmart's requirements, and he must be replaced as soon as possible. You have shared your concerns about Goodwrench with Mr. Wizard and his responses to your e-mails and private memos about it suggest he agrees with you.

Mr. Wizard

You are conflicted. You want to depart for Silicon Valley but in true engineering spirit you believe that no one can understand the product as you do. You're probably right about that. You are adamant that you must retain technical control until the Walmart opportunity is secured and the outsourcing is launched, at the very least. You are unmoving on the point that you will remain as Vice President of Engineering until those two milestones are met.

At the moment, you are keeping to yourself certain disturbing information about Ms. Winfrey. She has made it known to you in company e-mails and other memos (sent only to you) that she thinks Mr. Goodwrench is too old for his job, and that he should be "put out to pasture with the other old warhorses" as she said in one e-mail. Interestingly, you are inclined to agree—you think that Mr. Goodwrench has not kept up with new manufacturing techniques and he may not be the best person for the second generation Operations position.

Instructors: See Chapter 6 for additional facts which will introduce unexpected issues requiring urgent attention. These new issues can be introduced from time to time at your discretion.

Session 3: Goodbye Yellow Brick Road—5-member team
BACKGROUND

Smartfence survived the toxic spill, thanks to the supplier, who stepped up and provided interim facilities while the defect was repaired. Six months later, the company projects $15 million in sales, with the possibility of franchising and outsourcing. The company now has 100 employees. Walmart is interested in a modified product that could be sold to households, and suggests the possibility of selling 10,000 units annually, but requires a 60 percent reduction in price the first year and a 5 percent price reduction each of the succeeding three years.

The Company is targeting an IPO (initial public offering) in nine to twelve months. If the IPO is successful, Mr. Wizard may be able to depart with his cash, and buy that home on the ridge in Los Gatos. Mr. Goodwrench may be able to retire earlier than he had hoped. Ms. Winfrey, who dropped her secret plan to pursue a severance package (did she tell everyone about that?), sees big dollar signs as she rides the wave to global prominence. Mr. Donaghy is very well aware of the need to bring in the right skills to execute the IPO, but is frustrated with his colleagues' apparent inability to understand the strategic implications of the staffing issues. Mr. Moneypenny dreams of empire—legions of accountants and financial analysts, all reporting to him. All depends upon a successful IPO.

The Board reviewed advice from a prominent consultant:

The Company has reached that point in the growth of a business in which you need to bring in the "I have done this before" managers. This is not the time to reinvent the wheel because the failure to execute crisply in the next year could very likely result in the loss of business partners and customers, and make an IPO all but impossible. As this Company moves from a "few Chiefs, many Indians" structure to a layered management structure, it will undergo some severe organizational stress. Bringing in the second generation of management may require you to tell the loyal, hard-working, early-stage people that their career tracks are limited or have to be redirected. It is tough to do this to someone who took early-stage risk, did all-nighters for long stretches of time, did whatever had to be done to make the enterprise successful. This is why you have to make sure that the early stagers have an adequate stock position in the company. Speaking of stock, how will you attract the quality second-generation management types? The Securities and Exchange Commission looks very carefully at stock and option grants in the twelve months before the IPO. If the price of these grants does not ramp up toward the expected IPO price, the SEC may make the company re-price the stock grants and take charges to earnings, which can kill an IPO. This ramp up requirement will limit this Company's ability to use "cheap stock" to attract good people. With the lag time to find and recruit quality managers, it will most likely be a minimum of three to six months before most of them can be on the job. There won't be much time to integrate them into the business, continue to grow the business, and still hit a 9 to 12 month IPO target.

As the Company gets closer to the IPO the senior management team, which has been the driving force behind the Company's growth and which has the contacts with the strategic partners, will be diverted into financing issues and IPO. This will leave a management gap at just the time when extra attention will be required to manage the assimilation of the new people and channel the resulting "culture shift." Hey nobody said this stuff was easy.[2]

The Board members understand that it is time to review the current and future staffing needs, and to create a "now" and "later" organization chart for their areas of responsibility. Each of the founders must define the strategic needs of his or her area and to discuss the backgrounds and skill sets of the current team as they related to meeting these needs.

Record what emerges from your strategies and skills review, taking into account:

1. The Founders are talented, hard-working, and loyal; after all they have grown the business to $15M. But are the Founders capable of taking the Company to the next level? What qualifications and skills do they need to manage an IPO?

2. If the Founders divert their focus to the IPO, who will run the Company for the next nine months during the IPO?

3. Assuming the IPO is successful, will the Founders be capable of managing the Company after it goes public? What qualifications and skills will they need to manage a publicly-traded company?

4. Assuming one or more of the Founders will not survive the IPO because they can't (or won't) step up to new responsibilities, how should they be incentivized to leave?

5. How will the post-IPO second generation managers be compensated?

6 and 7. Other issues that may emerge during the Board meeting.

CHARACTER FACTS

Mr. Donaghy

You want to come out of this meeting with an agreement among the Founders regarding their current and future staffing needs. The current management team, of which they are the core, will be more and more engaged in the IPO and less and less focused on running the business. It takes several months to recruit and hire high-level, high-quality people. Trying to hire new people while launching an IPO will be a huge challenge for the organization. In addition, as they transition to a publicly-owned company, the organization will undergo severe organizational stress. You are worried about having enough value in the company to attract next-generation managers with stock options while also preserving adequate value for the Founders. You find it maddening that the other Founders can't seem to understand what's at stake; they keep focusing on the longer term strategies (which are important of course) but they don't seem to get the idea that without the right people at the right time, there won't be anyone around to execute those strategies!

Mr. Goodwrench

You are keen to supervise the handover to the second-generation team but not prepared to relinquish your position for another three years. You are excited about the prospect of learning new manufacturing techniques and the opportunity to start new manufacturing operations overseas. You insist that expansion must be led by experienced investment bankers and marketing professionals even though they must be paid more than Ms. Winfrey. You argue that too much is at stake to risk it all on an untested marketing guru, no matter how brilliant she may be. You think the talk of franchising is silly and distracting from the IPO, and don't want to spend any time on it.

Mr. Moneypenny

You plan to be the CFO of Smartfence until you drop dead at your desk many, many years from now. You think all marketing people are overpaid anyway (they don't really do anything except hire consultants to make pretty PowerPoint presentations with full color graphics) and you are willing to retain Ms. Winfrey and leave her in charge of marketing because she is paid less than more experienced marketing professionals. You are absolutely convinced that franchising is the way to go for two reasons: first, less capital is required, and second, following from the first point, less capital will be needed in the IPO—leaving more control in the Founders' hands. You acknowledge that vertical integration, including outsourcing to foreign manufacturing, would generate higher returns but point out that the risk is proportionately greater.

Ms. Winfrey

You are in this for the long haul. You see the opportunity for exponential growth, and have no intention of relinquishing your position as marketing goddess. You recognize the need for additional skills at the executive level with respect to the other Founders, but believe your own recent education at a top-flight business school is appropriately current for what is required. You think Mr. Goodwrench is an old fuddy-duddy who will stand in the way of implementing the cost-reduction methods you must embrace to meet Walmart's requirements, and he must be replaced as soon as possible. You have shared your concerns about Goodwrench with Mr. Wizard and his responses to your e-mails and private memos about it suggest he agrees with you.

Mr. Wizard

You are conflicted. You want to depart for Silicon Valley but in true engineering spirit you believe that no one can understand the product as you do. You're probably right about that. You are adamant that you must retain technical control until the Walmart opportunity is secured and the outsourcing is launched, at the very least. You are unmoving on the point that you will remain as Vice President of Engineering until those two milestones are met.

At the moment, you are keeping to yourself certain disturbing information about Ms. Winfrey. She has made it known to you in company e-mails and other memos (sent only to you) that she thinks Mr. Goodwrench is too old for his job, and that he should be "put out to pasture with the other old warhorses" as she said in one e-mail. Interestingly, you are inclined to agree—you think that Mr. Goodwrench has not kept up with new manufacturing techniques and he may not be the best person for the second generation Operations position.

Instructors: See Chapter 6 for additional facts which will introduce unexpected issues requiring urgent attention. These new issues can be introduced from time to time at your discretion.

Session 4: How Do You Sleep at Night?—4-member team

BACKGROUND

Smartfence has decided to postpone the IPO, given the urgent and troubling issues which recently surfaced. Given the environmental accident, plus two open investigations concerning ethical matters (allegations of embezzlement and employment discrimination), the Founders concluded that an IPO now would at best undervalue the stock, and at worst would fail and so taint the company that an IPO would never be feasible. You conclude that the best strategy would be to ensure the environmental issues were truly resolved and cooperate with the authorities with respect to the allegations.

At the last Board meeting, Mr. Moneypenny was suspended with pay and the Comptroller assumed his operational responsibilities pending resolution of the investigation; Mr. Moneypenny continued to serve as an advisor to the Board but his voting privileges were suspended. However, just before the start of this meeting the outside auditors submitted their final report concerning the allegations against Mr. Moneypenny. They have concluded that the questionable expenditures (hot tub, wine and beer, and the yellow Vespa) were all appropriately incurred on the company's behalf. The items were acquired for the company's use and consumption at its offsite retreat and hunting lodge. The auditors will close this investigation.

Ms. Winfrey and the company have acknowledged to the government the inappropriate e-mails which surfaced at the last Board meeting; however, as there was no evidence of actual harm to Mr. Goodwrench or any other member of a protected class Ms. Winfrey, the company, and the government have agreed to a plan which will resolve this matter. Ms. Winfrey will forfeit the right to receive any dividends or bonuses for two years; the company will pay all the government's expenses associated with the investigation; the company will provide ethics training for all its employees with

Warut Prathaksithorn/Shutterstock.com

particular emphasis on employment discrimination, and the company will provide the substantive contents of such training and the attendance records for government audit; the government will close the investigation.

The Board members are meeting today to review a recent internal investigation on a new issue. A female employee, in the Operations group, Ms. Crawford, has been accused by several coworkers of various improper activities including: (1) time card fraud; (2) misappropriation of company property; (3) fraudulent expense report claims. In addition, these employees have alleged that the head of Operations, Mr. Goodwrench, and his acting Deputy, Mr. Wizard, have known all along about these activities and have condoned them by their actions up to and including signing off on the fraudulent time cards and expense reports. The company's General Counsel has compiled an attorney–client privileged report describing the findings to date, which you may request. The Board will review the findings and decide how to deal with the situation. You are mindful that you have just closed two active ethics matters. You are concerned about your standing with the United States Government in particular and about the ethical culture of the company in general.

Review the findings, identify the issues, and record your decisions as to what actions the company will take. Give your reasons. Address, at a minimum, the employee, the coworkers, Mr. Goodwrench, and Mr. Wizard.

CHARACTER FACTS

Mr. Goodwrench

You know your job is at risk. You knew of the employee unrest in the group, but you relied on Mr. Wizard to deal with it. He's the one who signs time cards and expense reports as submitted to him and does not check the underlying assertions. He's the one who says that the reason for apparent discrepancies associated with Crawford's time cards and entry and exit records from the badge readers is that she doesn't always enter and exit the same buildings. You're not responsible for this. You don't want to do it, but maybe you have to throw Wizard under the bus.

Mr. Moneypenny

You expected to be fully exonerated with respect to the allegations against you, but you are disappointed that your colleagues doubted your honesty. Consequently, you feel no constraints to advancing your view that the Crawford situation must be dealt with crisply and firmly. She broke the law, she violated company rules and policies, her actions resulted in false claims to the government, and she must be terminated. The government must also be informed of her actions and the company's actions to correct her false claims.

Ms. Winfrey

You understand that the company's reputation for ethical conduct is hanging by a thread. You think it would be right for the company to act decisively, thus demonstrating responsible enforcement of the company's code of conduct—but unfortunately, your own conduct compromised the company in the first instance. It's awkward to promote rigorous enforcement with respect to others, when you just cut a deal in your own favor. Maybe you can argue for vigorous enforcement to demonstrate how committed you really are to the ethics program—you drank the Kool-Aid. And you can't help but wonder why Goodwrench and Wizard didn't do something about Crawford. Is there something going on that they haven't disclosed? Is something going on with Wizard . . . and Crawford? Surely not.

Mr. Wizard

You wonder what all the fuss is about. Crawford is a midlevel employee who does as she's told, and takes care of her assignments. These can even include picking up your dry-cleaning when you don't have time to do it. Isn't it better for the company and for the government that you focus on the important things and not waste his time on trivial distractions? Anyway, those women who kept the desk logs are just jealous of Crawford. That's obvious to anyone.

Instructors: See Chapter 6 for additional facts which will introduce unexpected issues requiring urgent attention. These new issues can be introduced from time to time at your discretion.

Session 4: How Do You Sleep at Night?—5-member team

BACKGROUND

Smartfence has decided to postpone the IPO, given the urgent and troubling issues that recently surfaced. Given the environmental accident, plus two open investigations concerning ethical matters (allegations of embezzlement and employment discrimination), the Founders concluded that an IPO now would at best under-value the stock, and at worst would fail and so taint the company that an IPO would never be feasible. You conclude that the best strategy would be to ensure the environmental issues were truly resolved and cooperate with the authorities with respect to the allegations.

At the last Board meeting, Mr. Moneypenny was suspended with pay and the Comptroller assumed his operational responsibilities pending resolution of the investigation; Mr. Moneypenny continued to serve as an advisor to the Board but his voting privileges were suspended. However, just before the start of this meeting the outside auditors submitted their final report concerning the allegations against Mr. Moneypenny. They have concluded that the questionable expenditures (hot tub, wine and beer, and the yellow Vespa) were all appropriately incurred on the company's behalf. The items were acquired for the company's use and consumption at its offsite retreat and hunting lodge. The auditors will close this investigation.

Ms. Winfrey and the company have acknowledged to the government the inappropriate e-mails which surfaced at the last Board meeting; however, as there was no evidence of actual harm to Mr. Goodwrench or any other member of a protected class Ms. Winfrey, the company, and the government have agreed to a plan which will resolve this matter. Ms. Winfrey will forfeit the right to receive any dividends or bonuses for two years; the company will pay all the government's expenses associated with the investigation; the company will provide ethics training for all its employees with particular emphasis on employment discrimination, and the company will provide the substantive contents of such training and the attendance records for government audit; the government will close the investigation.

The Board members are meeting today to review a recent internal investigation on a new issue. A female employee, in the Operations group, Ms. Crawford, has been accused by several coworkers of various improper activities including: (1) time card fraud; (2) misappropriation of company property; (3) fraudulent expense report claims. In addition, these employees have alleged that the head of Operations, Mr. Goodwrench, and his acting Deputy, Mr. Wizard, have known all along about these activities and have condoned them by their actions up to and including signing off on the fraudulent time cards and expense reports. The company's General Counsel has compiled an attorney–client privileged report describing the findings to date, which you may request. The Board will review the findings and decide how to deal with the situation. You are mindful that you have just closed two active ethics matters. You are concerned about your standing with the United States Government in particular and about the ethical culture of the company in general.

Review the findings, identify the issues and record your decisions as to what actions the company will take. Give your reasons. Address, at a minimum, the employee, the coworkers, Mr. Goodwrench, and Mr. Wizard.

CHARACTER FACTS

Mr. Donaghy

You are bitterly disappointed with your colleagues. Goodwrench and Wizard have demonstrated terrible judgment. The consequences of this matter will resonate beyond this boardroom and this meeting. Because of the false claims, even though the amounts of money are small, the government will mistrust the company. A broad ethical training program touching all employees and teaching the basics of time charging must be developed and deployed very quickly. The program will be expensive and will be distracting from everyone's regular duties. You are adamant that Crawford must be terminated for cause immediately. That doesn't bother you. What bothers you is what to do about Goodwrench and Wizard. Why didn't they do something about Crawford? Is there something going on that they haven't disclosed? Is something going on with Wizard . . . and Crawford? Surely not.

Mr. Goodwrench

You know your job is at risk. You knew of the employee unrest in the group, but you relied on Mr. Wizard to deal with it. He's the one who signs time cards and expense reports as submitted to him and does not check the underlying assertions. He's the one who says that the reason for apparent discrepancies associated with Crawford's time cards and entry and exit records from the badge readers is that she doesn't always enter and exit the same buildings. You're not responsible for this. You don't want to do it, but maybe you have to throw Wizard under the bus.

Mr. Moneypenny

You expected to be fully exonerated with respect to the allegations against you, but you are disappointed that your colleagues doubted your honesty. Consequently, you feel no constraints to advancing your view that the Crawford situation must be dealt with crisply and firmly. She broke the law, she violated company rules and policies, her actions resulted in false claims to the government, and she must be terminated. The government must also be informed of her actions and the company's actions to correct her false claims.

Ms. Winfrey

You understand that the company's reputation for ethical conduct is hanging by a thread. You think it would be right for the company to act decisively, thus demonstrating responsible enforcement of the company's code of conduct—but unfortunately, your own conduct compromised the company in the first instance. It's awkward to promote rigorous enforcement with respect to others, when you just cut a deal in your own favor. Maybe you can argue for vigorous enforcement to demonstrate how committed you really are to the ethics program, that you drank the Kool-Aid.

Mr. Wizard

You wonder what all the fuss is about. Crawford is a midlevel employee who does as she's told, and takes care of her assignments. These can even include picking up your dry-cleaning when you don't have time to do it. Isn't it better for the company and for the government that you focus on the important things and not waste his time on trivial distractions? Anyway, those women who kept the desk logs are just jealous of Crawford. That's obvious to anyone.

Instructors: See Chapter 6 for additional facts which will introduce unexpected issues requiring urgent attention. These new issues can be introduced from time to time at your discretion.

ENDNOTES

1. Hadzima, Joe. "Do You Still Have the Right People (In the Right Job)?" MIT. http://www.mitef. org/s/1314/interior-2-col.aspx?sid=1314&gid=5&pgid=5792

2. Id.

CHAPTER 4

Law, Society, and the Constitution: Judgment Day

Chapter Learning Objectives

After completing this chapter, students should be able to:

- Identify ethical decision-making frameworks, including the learning and practicing of multiple models for ethical decision making, by analyzing contemporary ethical and social issues from a strategic standpoint and addressing the tradeoffs faced by practicing managers.

- Consider responsibilities for ethical leadership that exist in contemporary organizations.

- Use legal reasoning to evaluate case information.

- Use critical thinking skills to extrapolate from the examples to other potential business issues.

- Define ethics and evaluate business strategies based on ethical principles.

Rules of the Game

> "Believing with you that religion is a matter which lies solely between man and his god . . . I contemplate with sovereign reverence that act of the whole American people which declared that their 'legislature' should 'make no law respecting an establishment of religion, or prohibiting the free exercise thereof,' thus building a wall of separation between church and State."
>
> Thomas Jefferson, *Letter to the Danbury Baptist Church,* Jan. 1, 1802
>
>
> "The government of the United States is not in any sense founded on the Christian religion."
>
> Treaty of Tripoli, Art. XI. Signed by Pres. John Adams. Ratified by the U.S. Senate June 10, 1797. Ratified by the United States June 10, 1797.
> —George Washington

Money. Family. Taxes. Duty. Freedom. Religion. Equality. Right to life. Right to die. What do these ideas have in common? Each of them has been the subject of adjudication in the courts of the United States. The general public may be aware of certain high-profile Supreme Court cases that address these ideas: *Roe v. Wade* and *Brown v. Board of Education*, for example. Supreme Court cases seem far removed from the daily lives of most of us, and as ordinary citizens we are much more likely to interact with local governmental entities and local regulation than to be a party in a Supreme Court case. Yet it is these local interactions involving ordinary citizens that form the basis of so many landmark decisions. Who was Roe in *Roe v. Wade*? Who was Brown in *Brown v. Board of Education*? Why did they participate in these now-famous cases? How did the actions of otherwise obscure individuals become the subject of constitutional law making? When we study law, we tend to focus on big issues and we spend comparatively little time exploring the origins of disputes at the local level. However, it is at the origin of the dispute that mistakes are made, opportunities are missed, and ethics lapse.

In Chapter 4, you will examine a particular dispute from its origin through its resolution in the federal courts of the United States. You will research the grant of authority to a local democratically elected entity and you will consider the limits on that authority. You will evaluate the actions of citizens and elected representatives in the context of ethical choices. You will examine in detail how actions of a local political entity can become the subject of a constitutional dispute and how the legal system dispositions a constitutional claim. You will learn about the litigation process, including substantive and procedural law, by re-enacting a portion of the court proceedings in an abbreviated form of a mock trial.

The case, *Kitzmiller v. Dover*,[1] provides a unique opportunity to review the progression of events culminating in a federal court trial because so much of the underlying conflict from the very beginning, long before anyone appeared in court, is a matter of public record. In this case, residents of a small town in Pennsylvania named Dover sued their local school board, alleging that a policy adopted by the board regarding the teaching of evolution—or more accurately the teaching of a purported scientific theory called "intelligent design"—in high school biology class was an establishment of religion prohibited by the First Amendment to the United States Constitution.

You will begin by individually researching the responsibilities of the school board. Next, each student will be randomly assigned to one of three teams: (1) citizens in favor of the policy; (2) citizens opposed to the policy; (3) panel of judges. You will view a documentary that examines how the controversy arose as well as the trial of the dispute in federal court. After viewing the documentary, you will complete certain assignments as if you were a participant in the case. Each student-citizen team will prepare a Memorandum of Law in support of its position. Each student-citizen team will select representatives who will orally present the team's position in Oral Summation to the court. The student-judges will hear the Oral Summations and prepare a Memorandum of Opinion that will resolve the case.

Grading

The standard grading scale applies. A = Excellent; B = Good; C = Adequate; D = Below average but passing; F = Failing. In order to earn a "B" grade a student will submit all written assignments, complete and on time, and will participate in and actively contribute to group activities. All written assignments will reflect proper organization and proofreading, and will identify sources. Submissions with incomplete sentences, improper grammar, or misspelled words will be returned without a grade.

CHAPTER ORGANIZATION

Responsibilities of the School Board

Team Assignments; NOVA Documentary "Judgment Day: Intelligent Design on Trial"[2]

Memorandum of Law; Memorandum of Opinion

Oral Summation to the Court

Memorandum of Opinion

Review and Debrief

Responsibilities of the School Board

In Dover, certain school board members took actions based on their personal beliefs which eventually resulted in a lawsuit against the school board on constitutional grounds. In order to understand whether the school board's actions were proper it is necessary to first understand the board's responsibilities. The Pennsylvania state legislature establishes local school boards and defines their responsibilities. Research how school boards work in Pennsylvania, addressing the following issues: the board's relationship with the community; the board's authority to dictate academic course content; guidance for ethical behavior when personal convictions conflict with positions taken by the board; authority of individual board members acting as individuals.[3] Summarize your findings in one-to-two typed pages. Identify your sources for future reference in subsequent assignments; the papers will be graded and returned to you.

Team Assignments; NOVA Documentary "Judgment Day: Intelligent Design on Trial"

The Dover school board adopted a policy that changed the science curriculum and required the school to read a statement in biology class denigrating evolution and promoting consideration of alternatives to evolution. Some residents of Dover opposed the actions of the Board and some supported them. Each student will be randomly assigned a role as a Dover resident in favor of the policy, a Dover resident opposed to the policy, or as a judge on the panel of judges. The class will view the NOVA documentary film "Judgment Day: Intelligent Design on Trial" together. The film is an in-depth look at the *Kitzmiller v. Dover* case. It includes trial reenactments based on the actual trial transcripts, commentary from litigants, teachers, and school board members, and insights into the community polarized by the lawsuit.[4]

Memorandum of Law; Memorandum of Opinion

Each student-resident team will prepare a Memorandum of Law in support of that team's position. For this assignment, the term Memorandum of Law means a written memorandum of issues and supporting legal arguments. It is similar to a legal brief prepared by an attorney for submission in litigation, but without procedural formalities required by rules of court. Your Memorandum of Law will articulate why you think the panel of judges should decide the case in your favor. You will identify the dispositive issues and supporting legal arguments, with specific reference to the evidence presented at trial, including testimony given in the NOVA re-enactment, the trial transcript, and exhibits.[5] The Memorandum of Law is a graded assignment. A template for the Memorandum of Law is included at the end of this chapter.

The student judges will prepare a Draft Memorandum of Opinion. For this assignment, a Memorandum of Opinion means a written statement by the court announcing the court's ruling on the issues. Your Memorandum of Opinion will include the ruling on each issue and identify the law and the facts upon which the court's ruling is founded. Factual findings must be supported by evidence presented at trial, which will include your assessments of witness credibility and other factors that the court finds persuasive; including testimony given in the NOVA re-enactment, the trial transcript, and exhibits.[6] The Draft Memorandum of Opinion is based upon the issues and evidence that the judges expect the parties to present in the Summation; after the Oral Summation, the Draft will be finalized as described in more detail below. A template for the Memorandum of Opinion is included at the end of this chapter.

Oral Summation to the Court

One or more representatives of each student-resident team will present an Oral Summation of their case to the court. For this assignment, Oral Summation means an oral review of the issues and the evidence presented during the trial, and an argument as to why the court should find in favor of your position. The summation is the litigant's last opportunity to persuade the trier of fact to rule in the litigant's favor. In *Kitzmiller v. Dover* the parents as plaintiffs bear the burden of proof so they will present their summation first, and the team supporting the policy will go last. The Oral Summation is a graded assignment. A template for the Oral Summation is included at the end of this chapter.

Memorandum of Opinion

After hearing the Oral Summations, the student judges will finalize their Memorandum of Opinion and will present it to the class. The Memorandum of Opinion is a graded assignment. A template for the Memorandum of Opinion is included at the end of this chapter.

Review and Debrief

The class will review the exercise in a collective debriefing.

Template: Memorandum of Law

Times New Roman 12, double-spaced, number pages bottom right

Format:

Heading (The proper heading is provided below for your information and use).

1.   Issue #1:

(a)   Issue #1: Describe the issue in one question.

(b)   Answer: Answer the question presented by the Issue statement, in a concise response beginning with either "Yes" or "No."

(c)   Discussion: Explain why your Answer in 1(b) is correct. Identify the legal principles and facts that support your position from the evidence introduced at trial.

(d)   Conclusion: Offer a strong and compelling statement that summarizes why your position should prevail.

2.   Issue #2:

Repeat (a) – (d) for each Issue.

See example below:

Heading:

UNITED STATES DISTRICT COURT

M.D. PENNSYLVANIA

TAMMY KITZMILLER, et al.,	)	
Plaintiffs,	)	
v.	)	**Civil Action No. 04cv2688**
DOVER AREA SCHOOL DISTRICT, et al.,	)	
Defendants	)	
_____	)	

1

MEMORANDUM OF LAW

1. Plaintiffs' standing

    a. Should any of the Plaintiffs in the case be dismissed because they lack standing to sue?

    b. No. The Plaintiffs' children are all affected by the ID Policy adopted by the Board, even though some of them are too young for high school and some have already passed beyond the ninth grade in which the ID Policy would be carried out.

    c. Plaintiffs' children range in age from kindergarten to twelfth grade. Defendants argue that the claims of the parents whose children are not yet old enough for ninth grade are not ripe for adjudication, and therefore those parents lack standing to sue and their claims should be dismissed. Defendants also argue that the claims of the parents whose children have already passed ninth grade are moot, and therefore those parents lack standing to sue and their claims should be dismissed. The case law regarding violations of the Establishment Clause in schools has never required proof of immediate classroom impact to establish standing to challenge prohibited conduct. While ninth grade students are most immediately affected, enacting a policy in violation of the Establishment Clause is a constitutional injury to the entire school community.

    d. Defendants' Motions for Dismissal based on lack of standing should be denied. None of the cases cited by Defendants limits standing to only those students immediately subjected to the prohibited policy, such as the ninth grade biology students in this case. The entire school community is harmed by conduct prohibited by the Establishment Clause.

1

2.	Issue #2

	a.

	b.

	c.

	d.

3.	Et al.

Template: Oral Summation

Time allowed for each side: 10 minutes

Plaintiffs present their summation first.

Judges may ask questions, which must be answered.

Format:

1. "May it please the Court?"

2. Introduce yourself.

3. Tell the Court what you want them to do: i.e., "find in favor of plaintiffs" or "reject plaintiffs' claims and find in favor of defendants"

4. Why? (your theory of the case, developed in your Memorandum of Law)

5. Highlight facts from your perspective

6. Conclusion: forceful but short, what do you want the Court to do?

1

Template: Memorandum of Opinion

Times New Roman 12, double-spaced, number pages bottom right

Format:

Heading (The proper heading is provided below for your information and use).

1. Issue #1:

    (a) Issue #1: Describe the issue in one question.

    (b) Holding: State the court's holding on the issue.

    (c) Discussion: Explain the legal principles and facts that support your holding.

2. Issue #2:

    Repeat (a) – (c) for all Issues.

Heading:

UNITED STATES DISTRICT COURT

M.D. PENNSYLVANIA

TAMMY KITZMILLER, et al.,)	
Plaintiffs,)	
v.)	**Civil Action No. 04cv2688**
DOVER AREA SCHOOL DISTRICT, et al.,)	
Defendants)	
_____)	

MEMORANDUM OF OPINION

HOLDINGS:

1.   Plaintiffs' standing

    a.   Defendants have moved for dismissal of certain defendants based on lack of standing.

    b.   Defendants' Motions for Dismissal based on lack of standing are DENIED.

    c.   The Plaintiffs all have standing to sue. No cases have required proof of immediate classroom impact to establish standing to challenge prohibited conduct. All the Plaintiffs' children are affected by the ID Policy adopted by the Board, even though some of them are too young for high school and some have already passed beyond the ninth grade in which the ID Policy would be carried out. Enacting a policy in violation of the Establishment Clause is a constitutional injury to the entire school community. The entire school community is harmed by conduct prohibited by the Establishment Clause.

2.   Issue #2

    a.

    b.

    c.

3.   Et al.

1

Endnotes

1. *Tammy Kitzmiller, et al. v. Dover Area School District, et al.*, 400 F. Supp. 2d 707 (M.D. Pa. 2005).

2. NOVA. "Judgment Day: Intelligent Design on Trial," NOVA website, http://www.pbs.org/wgbh/nova/id/; also available on DVD in the campus library. Run time 1:52:21.

3. The Pennsylvania School Boards Association (PSBA) maintains a comprehensive website for its members, the local school boards such as the Dover board, including a Code of Conduct for board members and standards for effective school governance. See Pennsylvania School Boards Association. https://www.psba.org. The PSBA also publishes "How to Run for School Board" which includes the Code of Conduct and standards of governance. To see the Code of Conduct and governance standards, go to www.psba.org; click on Resources at the bottom of the landing page, then "How to Run for School Board" in the right-hand column, or paste this URL into your browser: https://www.psba.org/resources/run-school-board-guide-school-board candidates-Pennsylvania/.

4. In addition to the documentary, NOVA's program website provides a number of links offering information related to the issues in the case. A transcript of the documentary is also available on the website. The NOVA website is found at: http://www.pbs.org/wgbh/nova/id/.

5. A complete, indexed trial transcript is available online at: National Center for Science Education. "Kitzmiller v. Dover: Intelligent Design on Trial," http://ncse.com/creationism/legal/kitzmiller-trial-transcripts. In addition to the indexed trial transcript, the NCSE website provides copies of motions and orders, transcripts of arguments in pretrial hearings, copies of some exhibits, and links to other associated information.

6. Ibid.

CHAPTER 5

Ethics Programs in Practice: United Technologies Case Study

Chapter Learning Objectives

After completing this chapter, students should be able to:

- Define ethics and evaluate business strategies based on ethical principles.

- Explain a business organization's role in social responsibility.

- Recognize responsibilities for ethical leadership that exist in contemporary organizations.

- Recognize the principles and practices of responsible corporate governance.

Rules of the Game

Assume for this exercise that we all agree we need ethics programs in our business enterprises. How would you go about designing and deploying an ethics program? Perhaps you would retain an expert to assist you. That's a good idea, but how will you know whether the expert's advice is right for your enterprise? And after you launch your ethics program, how will you measure its effectiveness?

This case study follows the evolution of an ethics program from inception to maturity at United Technologies Corporation. Each of its five sections describes a significant milestone in the development of the company's ethics program. The reading provides information not only about the company's actions but also describes the external context in which those actions were taken. At the end of each section, you will consider the choices the company made as well as the context, and answer a series of questions before moving on to the next section.

CHAPTER ORGANIZATION

Background

Defense Industry Initiative and UTC's Policy Statement

A Comprehensive Ethics Program: The Federal Sentencing Guidelines and UTC's Code of Ethics

Creating an Ethical Culture: Sarbanes-Oxley and UTC's ACE Program

Sustaining an Ethical Culture

UTC Subsidiaries Plead Guilty to Export Violations

Background

United Technologies Corporation (NYSE: UTX) ("UTC") is a diversified company providing products and services to the aerospace and building industries worldwide. The company's antecedents are in the defense industry in the 1920s with the formation of Pratt & Whitney Aircraft. UTC's aerospace businesses grew to include Pratt & Whitney's aircraft propulsion, Sikorsky Aircraft, and the design, manufacture, and service businesses of UTC Aerospace Systems. UTC's Building and Industrial Systems businesses include Otis elevators and escalators, Carrier air conditioning, and a broad range of fire safety and security technologies. In 2013, UTC reported $62.6 billion net sales with 212,400 employees.[1]

On October 28, 2010, United Technologies Corporation and Louis Chenevert, then UTC's Chairman and CEO, received the Stanley C. Pace Ethics and Leadership Award. The *Pace* award is presented annually by the Ethics Resource Center to "an individual, or group of individuals, recognized as having unwavering integrity and having demonstrated moral vision and the ability to translate that vision into specific goals."[2] The announcement accompanying the award applauded UTC for applying to ethics the same discipline and quantitative rigor that it applies to other business initiatives and for systematically evaluating and rewarding ethical conduct at all levels of the company. Ethics, said Chenevert, are the foundation of UTC's performance culture.[3] Twenty years earlier, headlines about UTC were less likely to acclaim ethical achievements and more likely to allege fraud against the U.S. government. During the 1980s a number of companies providing defense hardware and services to the U.S. government were accused in highly publicized venues of fraud, waste, and abuse in the performance of their government contracts. The extensive record of one 1987 congressional hearing includes in a list of notorious allegations of defense contractor overcharging a $436.00 hammer, a $9,609.00 wrench, and a $7,400.00 coffee maker.[4] The accusations were made in government audit reports and investigative findings, and the more inflammatory accusations were widely reported in print and broadcast media and were the subjects of several late-night comedy skits. UTC was one of those defense contractors accused of wrongdoing through its business units Pratt & Whitney, Hamilton Standard, Sikorsky, and Norden Systems. The specific accusations against UTC included "lavishly entertaining" government officials,[5] overcharging on contract pricing,[6] and conspiring to divert funds intended for Israel.[7] The defense contractors' conduct was scrutinized not only in Congressional hearings and news articles but also in civil and criminal lawsuits.[8] Eventually they collectively would pay hundreds of millions of dollars in fines and reimbursements.

The 1980s defense procurement scandals prompted a reconsideration of corporate culture for many of the companies caught up in them. The principal measure of a savvy, nimble, competitive company was rate of return on the company's stock, very nearly to the exclusion of other metrics. The relentless discipline of maximizing shareholder value left little time for reflection about corporate culture and governance practices that appeared to have an attenuated and unquantified effect on the bottom line. But when defense industry contractors found themselves criticized by the Department of Defense, prosecuted by the Department of Justice, and humiliated in the eyes of the nation, their executive leadership rediscovered the language of moral agency and ethical responsibility.[9] It was not enough to merely distinguish lawful behavior from unlawful behavior. Frequently issues were ambiguous. Solutions required exercise of judgment. Sometimes it was necessary to ask not only "Can I . . . ?" but also to ask "Should I . . . ?" The evolution of formal, managed ethical culture as an attribute separate from (although related to) compliance with law had begun.

> **evolution**
>
> a process of gradual change over time toward a more complex and more desirable condition

> **ethical culture**
>
> used expansively, encompassing corporate policies, employee attitudes and behaviors, and internal structures and processes

In 1986, UTC adopted a corporate policy on contracting with the United States Government. In 1990, UTC launched its first comprehensive, company-wide Code of Ethics expanding to the whole corporation, including its commercial businesses, ethical norms developed in the government contract business units. In 2006, UTC made structural changes to its Ethical and Compliance Program and applied rigorous business process management tools to measure the effectiveness of its ethics initiatives. This case study explores the evolution of ethical culture in UTC since the 1980s focusing on those three specific corporate initiatives.

Defense Industry Initiative and UTC's Policy Statement

The pervasive fraud, waste, and abuse allegations of the 1980s provoked a variety of government responses.[10] An earlier General Accounting Office report had characterized the scope of defense industry-wide procurement fraud as "of critical proportions."[11] The Department of Defense, Office of Inspector General, created in 1982, established whistleblower hotlines and issued guidebooks on fraud to its thousands of auditors and investigators.[12] Offenses formerly treated as civil and therefore punishable only by civil fines were criminalized, and the Department of Justice aggressively sought criminal convictions. Offending contractors could also be barred from doing business with the Government either temporarily or permanently, in the form of suspension or debarment respectively. UTC was one of several targets of a government investigation called "Operation Ill Wind" launched in 1986, which resulted eventually in over ninety convictions of companies and individuals including sixteen of the top twenty defense contractors in the United States.[13]

President Reagan, concerned about the public's loss of confidence in the defense industry and in national security, appointed a commission to evaluate the issues and recommend reforms. This group came to be called the Packard Commission, named after its Chairman David Packard, co-founder of Hewlett-Packard.[14] The Commission's charter encompassed a broad array of Defense Department procurement issues, policies, and processes. Although the high-profile allegations of industry overcharging and mischarging were a comparatively insignificant cost element of the overall Defense Department procurement system, which was encumbered with inefficiencies from initial strategic planning to final spare parts procurements, negative public perception of defense contractors could not be disregarded. In its final report to the President in June 1986, the Packard Commission recommended that government contractors develop and vigilantly enforce written codes of ethics, including procedures for self-management, voluntary disclosure of wrong-doing, and employee reporting of misconduct without fear of retribution.[15]

The Defense Industry Initiative

Concurrently with the Packard Commission's work, defense industry companies themselves had developed a voluntary ethics and compliance program that incorporated formal ethical codes, self-audit, voluntary disclosure, and non-retaliation policies. Senior officials of eighteen defense contractors, among them UTC, formed a non-profit association of United States defense contractors which became known as the Defense Industry Initiative on Business Ethics and Conduct (the "DII"). The DII drafted and published a set of six guidelines that each member of the DII adopted, known as the DII Principles. The DII Principles were included in the Packard Commission's Final Report to the President. (See Exhibit A for the current DII Principles as updated March 2010). By July of 1986, thirty-two major defense contractors had signed and the membership now numbers seventy-seven defense contractors.[16] The six principles stated as follows:

1. Each Signatory shall have and adhere to a written code of business conduct. The code establishes the high ethical values expected for all within the Signatory's organization.

2. Each Signatory shall train all within the organization as to their personal responsibilities under the code.

3. Signatories shall encourage internal reporting of violations of the Code, with the promise of no retaliation for such reporting.

4. Signatories have the obligation to self-govern by implementing controls to monitor compliance with federal procurement laws and by adopting procedures for voluntary disclosure of violations of federal procurement laws to appropriate authorities.

5. Each Signatory shall have responsibility to each other to share their best practices in implementing the DII principles; each Signatory shall participate in an annual Best Practices Forum.

6. Each Signatory shall be accountable to the public.

UTC's Policy Statement

The DII Principles require each signatory to maintain and adhere to its own written code of conduct. In 1986 UTC published its Policy Statement on Business Ethics and Conduct in Contracting with the United States Government. The Policy Statement has been updated from time to time and is still in effect at UTC. The Introduction to the Policy Statement acknowledges the company's responsibility to deliver value to its shareholders, but also states that ethics, morality, and social responsibility take on added significance when doing business with the United States Government.[17] The Policy Statement addresses specific circumstances that typically arise in government contracting, but not in commercial contracts, such as handling classified national security information and submission of cost and pricing date. The Policy Statement provides, in part, as follows:

1. Our policy is to deliver quality products and services to the government at fair and reasonable prices.

2. We are committed to compliance with the letter and spirit of government contracting laws and regulations.

3. Government information that is national security classified shall not be accepted from any source, either directly or indirectly, in circumstances where there is reason to believe that the release is unauthorized.

4. We are prohibited by statute from soliciting or obtaining a competitor's proprietary information or the government's source selection information. UTC will not seek or accept, directly or indirectly, proprietary or source selection information regarding any government procurement. Following contract award, such information may be sought through requests made directly to the government, such as a request under the Freedom of Information Act.

5. Our employees shall not prepare any government solicitation, specification, or evaluation criteria and anonymously or surreptitiously submit it to the government.

6. We are frequently required to submit accounting and other records to the government as a basis for payment on existing contracts and in support of estimates on future contracts. It is our policy to charge all labor and material costs accurately to the appropriate account, regardless of the status of the budget for that account. Improprieties, such as charging labor or material costs improperly or to the wrong account, charging direct contract effort to an overhead or indirect account, and falsification of time cards or other records will not be tolerated.

7. We are required to submit cost or pricing data to the government and to certify that it is current, accurate, and complete. The definition of data that must be disclosed is very broad and includes facts but also management decisions, estimates (based on verifiable data), and other information that a reasonable person would expect to affect the negotiations. Our policy is full disclosure of complete and accurate cost and pricing data that is current up to the date of agreement on price.

8. We submit proposals to the government for reimbursement of costs. It is our policy to request reimbursement only for costs which are reasonable in amount and which are clearly allowable under

government regulations, or as to which we have a good-faith belief that the costs are allowable. For example, alcoholic beverages, promotional items (including models, souvenirs, and gifts), donations, or entertainment are expressly unallowable. Detailed guidance on cost allowability can be found in UTC's Employee Guide entitled "Allowability of Costs on U.S. Government Contracts."

9. We are often required to certify compliance with quality control specifications and testing requirements for our products. Our policy is to deliver goods that meet all contract requirements and give the customer the highest degree of confidence in our products. Improprieties, such as failure to conduct required testing, or manipulation of test procedures or data, will not be tolerated.

10. Government rules on gifts and gratuities (broadly defined to include entertainment and business meals) are very restrictive. Employees shall not offer or give a gift or gratuity to any government employee, except where clearly permitted by applicable government regulations (for example, 32 Code of Federal Regulations Part 40). Guidance with respect to the applicable regulations can be obtained from the operating unit Business Practices/Compliance Officer. Furthermore, employees shall not offer or give, directly or indirectly, anything to a government employee who is a procurement official or who performs a procurement function except: (a) beverages at a business meeting, (b) light snacks for a business meeting where government employees in travel status are in attendance, and (c) promotional items displaying the company logo and having a truly nominal value, such as baseball caps or pads of paper. Any exceptions must be approved in writing by the UTC Vice President, Business Practices.

11. Special restrictions apply to hiring or retaining as an employee or consultant, any government employee (other than secretarial, clerical, or similarly graded employees). There are many "revolving door" laws which apply to government employees and restrict their employment outside the government. In some cases, even discussions of possible employment are prohibited. Accordingly, clearance must be obtained from the operating unit or UTC General Counsel (as appropriate) before even mentioning proposed employment to such a current government employee, and before hiring or retaining any such former government employee who left the government within the three previous years. In addition, any plans to employ retired military officers of general or flag rank, or civilian officials having the rank of deputy assistant secretary or above, must be approved by the UTC Vice President, Business Practices.

12. Employees may not accept gifts, entertainment, or other gratuities from anyone seeking a contract with or purchase by UTC (in whatever form, including purchase orders or credit card purchases), other than customary business courtesies that are reasonable in frequency and value. (See the policy circular entitled "The Giving and Receiving of Business Gifts" for additional guidance.) Employees may not solicit any gift, entertainment, or other gratuity. Seeking or accepting any payment, gift, or other thing of value from a subcontractor, vendor, or supplier for the purpose of obtaining or acknowledging favorable treatment under a government contract or subcontract (a "kickback") is a crime.

13. Aside from the restrictions of paragraph 11, additional limitations apply to those employees who have direct purchasing responsibilities. This includes all employees in the purchasing department and others, if designated by the operating unit such that the affected employees can be readily identified. The additional designations could include, for example, employees who are supplier quality assurance representatives, employees responsible for source selections, or employees authorized to make credit card purchases. Such employees may only accept (a) beverages, light snacks, and business meals served during business meetings held at the facilities of subcontractors, vendors, or suppliers, (b) business meals when in travel status, (c) promotional or advertising items having a truly nominal value, such as baseball caps or pads of paper, and (d) any other gift, entertainment, or other gratuity if reported to and approved in writing by the Business Practices/Compliance Officer of the operating unit or by the UTC Vice President, Business Practices. Guidance with respect to this policy can be obtained from the operating unit Business Practices/Compliance Officer or the UTC Vice President, Business Practices.

14. Employees shall not offer or give entertainment, gifts, or gratuities to representatives or employees of higher tier government contractors other than customary business courtesies that are reasonable in frequency and value. Offering or giving any payment, gift, or other thing of value to such a person for the purpose of obtaining or acknowledging favorable treatment (a "kickback") is a crime.

15. Even though not otherwise prohibited, employees will not offer or give to any representative or employee of a higher tier government contractor any entertainment, gift, gratuity, or anything else of value that such representative or employee is known to be prohibited from accepting under the policies of the higher tier government contractor.

16. Consultants performing work related to a government contract or subcontract shall be required by contract to comply with the laws and regulations relating to government contracting and with this Policy Statement. This Policy Statement shall be incorporated in the standard terms and conditions for all such consultant contracts, and each such contract shall expressly provide for termination in the event the consultant violates either the laws or regulations relating to government contracting or this Policy Statement.

Questions

1. What are the essential elements of the DII principles?

2. Does UTC's *Policy Statement on Business Ethics and Conduct in Contracting with the United States Government* meet the commitments the company accepted when adopting the DII principles?

3. How can companies judge the practical usefulness of an ethics code?

A Comprehensive Ethics Program: The Federal Sentencing Guidelines and UTC's Code of Ethics

In November of 1991 the Federal Sentencing Guidelines for Organizations (the "Sentencing Guidelines") became effective.[18] The Sentencing Guidelines for Organizations apply to entities such as corporations, unions, trusts, and non-profits which are found guilty of felonies and Class A misdemeanors and are designed to further both "just punishment" and "deterrence" by levying fair and consistent sentences. According to the legal principle of *respondeat superior,* a corporation is responsible for its employee's wrongdoing, even if the employee's actions are prohibited by company policy; because of this corporate responsibility, "companies that worked hard to obey the law and ensure that employees did as well were often treated in the same way as organizations in which misconduct was not only tolerated but encouraged."[19] The Sentencing Guidelines addressed this disparity by providing that fines may be mitigated for companies that have developed and enforced internal codes of conduct. On the other hand, for companies without such codes of conduct, fines may be more severe. Adoption of a code of conduct remained a voluntary act on the part of the organization, as was the case with the DII. Amendments to the Sentencing Guidelines in 2004 and 2008 reinforced the expectation that the Board of Directors will be knowledgeable and active in implementing ethics programs, and will provide resources for implementation.[20]

An Effective Compliance and Ethics Program

Companies convicted of criminal conduct cannot be imprisoned, but can be fined, ordered to make restitution, and subjected to forfeiture penalties. If the company can demonstrate that it has an effective compliance and ethics program, as measured by seven criteria specified in Chapter 8 of the Guidelines, it is eligible to receive credit (i.e., mitigation of fines) pursuant to the Sentencing Guidelines:

1. The organization must have established compliance standards and procedures to be followed by its employees and other agents that are reasonably capable of reducing the prospect of criminal conduct.

2. Specific individual(s) within high-level personnel of the organization must have been assigned overall responsibility to oversee compliance with such standards and procedures.

3. The organization must have used due care not to delegate substantial discretionary authority to individuals whom the organization knew, or should have known through the exercise of due diligence, had a propensity to engage in illegal activities.

4. The organization must have taken steps to communicate effectively its standards and procedures to all employees and other agents, e.g., by requiring participation in training programs or by disseminating publications that explain in a practical manner what is required.

5. The organization must have taken reasonable steps to achieve compliance with its standards, e.g., by utilizing monitoring and auditing systems reasonably designed to detect criminal conduct by its employees and other agents and by having in place and publicizing a reporting system whereby employees and other agents could report criminal conduct by others within the organization without fear of retribution.

6. The standards must have been consistently enforced through appropriate disciplinary mechanisms, including, as appropriate, discipline of individuals responsible for the failure to detect an offense. Adequate discipline of individuals responsible for an offense is a necessary component of enforcement; however, the form of discipline that will be appropriate will be case-specific.

7. After an offense has been detected, the organization must have taken all reasonable steps to respond appropriately to the offense and to prevent further similar offenses— including any necessary modifications to its program to prevent and detect violations of law.[21]

The Sentencing Guidelines model reflects the defense industry experience from the 1980s.[22] In addition, the Sentencing Guidelines codified two significant developments in the evolution of ethical conduct then underway in U.S. businesses. First, the defense industry's adoption of the DII principles demonstrated that companies could and would voluntarily adopt ethics programs. Second, by rewarding businesses that do adopt effective ethics programs, the Sentencing Guidelines institutionalized ethics and compliance as a mainstream business objective.

UTC's leadership had also concluded by 1990 that an ethics program should not be confined to defense industry operations. UTC contemplated a more ambitious and comprehensive ethics program going far beyond its defense industry policy statement. UTC's goal was to build a uniform ethical culture across its entire operation. But any company-wide, universal initiative on ethics or any other issue would have to be designed and deployed taking into account UTC's particular corporate structure and demographics.

The Whole Is More than the Sum of Its Parts

In 1975 Harry Gray, then CEO of United Aircraft, changed the company's name to United Technologies, signaling anticipated diversification. At that time, the company included Pratt & Whitney, Hamilton Standard, and Sikorsky Helicopter, all government contractors with both government and commercial business. United Technologies acquired the commercial businesses Otis Elevator in 1976, and Carrier Corporation in 1979, followed by Sundstrand in 1999, Chubb Security in 2003, Kidde in 2005, and Rocketdyne in 2005. Since 1975,

UTC has been an industrial conglomerate encompassing powerful brands, and the business units themselves are formidable competitors in their respective industries as indicated in the following chart:[23]

Business Unit (2013)	Business Unit Net Sales (billions $)
Aerospace Systems	$13.3
Pratt & Whitney	$14.5
Sikorsky	$6.3
UTC Building and Industrial Systems *Includes Otis, Carrier, Chubb, Kidde*	$29.3
	$63.4

FIGURE 5.1

Because UTC's business units "derive little of their identity from UTC"[24] corporate initiatives driven by headquarters imperatives must respect the independence and self-management of the business units. A company-wide, universal ethics initiative with its roots in the defense industry could meet cultural resistance in the commercial business units which had been largely unaffected by the defense industry upheavals. In addition, the development of a universal ethics program would have to accommodate the diversity of UTC's workforce, representing many countries and speaking many languages,[25] and respect different cultural traditions.[26] It would take several years to develop a universal ethics and compliance culture perceived as organic to all the business units.

UTC Code of Ethics

In 1990, UTC first published its comprehensive Code of Ethics. The Code of Ethics institutionalized universal, company-wide standards of conduct, self-governance, and accountability. The Code of Ethics was more than a recitation of rules. It identified corporate values and commitments. It established a process for decision making.

Certain functions were centered at the business unit. The Code linked management objectives and rewards to compliance and gave the CEO of each business unit responsibility for implementation within the business unit. Existing structures for both open and confidential channels for reporting employee concerns were refined. Training programs were launched.

At the corporate level a Vice President is responsible for two implementing functions, the Ombuds/DIALOG program and the Business Practices program. The Ombuds/DIALOG program, first established in 1986, provides channels for communication that are confidential, neutral, and independent of local management.[27] The Ombudsmen are trained and available as intermediaries for complex issues, while the DIALOG process is intended for two-way communication on less complex matters. Employees can communicate their questions and concerns by phone, mail, or e-mail. Both these resources are available for circumstances under which the employee wishes to remain unidentified and both guarantee the employee's anonymity.

The business practices organization, also reporting to the corporate level Vice President, is responsible for overseeing policies, training, and investigations, and oversees compliance risk management and audit. As a corporate function the Business Practices office can assure equitable and consistent implementation across the corporation. The Business Practices office also oversees a network of approximately 450 Business Practices Officers (BPOs) who are located in local business units throughout the corporation. The BPOs all hold other positions within the company and assume BPO responsibilities on a part-time basis. Local employees can seek guidance on ethics issues from their local BPOs.

The company also defined a framework for decision making. This framework has been refined in more recent updates of the code, but the essential principles are largely unchanged. In seeking positive outcomes, UTC's process for decision making includes the following steps: (1) involving the right people, (2) understanding the facts, (3) understanding the legal requirements, (4) considering the duties owed to stakeholders and the impact of alternative decisions, (5) comparing alternatives with reference to company values, (6) making a tentative decision that is lawful and seems best, and (7) asking "Should I?"

Questions

1. How does the UTC *Code of Ethics* differ from the *Policy Statement on Business Ethics and Conduct in Contracting with the United States Government?*

2. UTC designed a system that defined values, established rules, authorized functions for reporting issues and concerns, and established a process for decision making. What issues might arise as a result of UTC's program design which is both (1) uniform and consistent across the company's global operations and (2) flexible to accommodate business unit and local practices?

3. Does the system defined and established by UTC's company-wide Code of Ethics satisfy the seven criteria of the Sentencing Guidelines?

Creating an Ethical Culture: Sarbanes-Oxley and UTC's ACE Program

UTC has delivered consistent, positive financial performance for many years. For example, for the ten-year period ending December 31, 2013, UTC returned 197 percent to the shareholders, almost twice the DJIA and the S&P 500.[28] One reason for the company's success is relentless focus on process management and continuous improvement. Each of UTC's business units is a manufacturer, and manufacturing operations generally are susceptible to improvement through process discipline. "That focus on process is one reason the company shuns financing and other businesses to which those skills don't apply, as well as businesses that simply have no pricing power. The focus on continuous improvement allows UTC to extract gains, even when times are tough."[29]

If You Can't Measure It, You Can't Manage It

UTC's continuous improvement methods are collectively known as "Achieving Competitive Excellence" ("ACE"). ACE has been described in the aggregate as a business operating system because it is based on a broad approach, uses specific tools, is supported by dedicated people and departments and is measured and rewarded. The system includes:[30]

Process Improvement and Elimination of Waste	Problem Solving
1. 5S—visual workplace	8. Market Feedback Analysis
2. Value Stream Management	9. QCPC (Quality Clinic Process Charting)
3. Process Control and Certification	10. Relentless Root Cause Analysis
4. Standard Work	11. Mistake Proofing
5. Production Preparation Process	
6. Total Productive Maintenance	**Decision Making**
7. Set-up Reduction	12. Passport Process

FIGURE 5.2

A thorough analysis of the ACE Operating System is located at http://www.utc.com/Our-Company/Our-Operating-System/Documents/UTC_ACE_CaseStudy.pdf.

The lean production and productivity improvement methods listed above are used in different forms by many production companies. At UTC, however, ACE is said to be more than a set of measurements; it is a corporate culture. Many at UTC attribute the company's financial performance through good times and bad to process improvements implemented through the use of ACE tools. According to former Chairman and CEO George David, the bulk of the productivity revolution at UTC came from process improvements, not product innovation, and from better processes, not better machines—"It's mostly a mindset."[31]

By the 1990s, UTC had in place the Code of Ethics, the Business Practices function and the BPOs, and the Ombuds/DIALOG program, collectively referred to as the Ethics and Compliance Program. UTC's culture of continuous process improvement led inevitably to a self-evaluation phase in the Ethics and Compliance Program in order to determine whether or not, and to what extent, the program was working, and how it could be improved. Raw data about the Ethics and Compliance Program in existence and available included the number of calls and inquiries to the Ombuds/DIALOG program, the types of issues presented in those calls and inquiries, the nature of the resolution of the issues, feedback from the BPOs and employee surveys.

The ACE tools were available, understood, and trusted. From 2001 forward, UTC continued to develop the ACE tools and apply them to functions and processes throughout the corporation, not just the manufacturing floor. It was a logical next step to apply those tools to the data available in the Ethics and Compliance program. Anonymous employee surveys tested employee awareness of the company's ethical programs. Reported concerns were categorized and grouped to measure recurrence and frequency. Process management tools were applied to test the integrity of the system channels.

SARBANES-OXLEY

In 2001 and 2002, while UTC was developing and deploying ACE tools across all of the company, shattering business failures at Enron, WorldCom, Tyco, and other marquee businesses, all involving notorious management misconduct, demonstrated that business ethics had not been fully institutionalized despite policy statements and ethics initiatives. The environment was described as a "bull market in scandals."[32] These frauds "destroyed or diminished the companies, and wreaked havoc on thousands of innocent individuals in the bargain. Among the collateral damage: hundreds of billions in shareholder value, tens of thousands of jobs, employee retirement funds eviscerated, and the erosion of public trust in big corporations and the financial markets that help sustain them."[33] These catastrophes occurred notwithstanding the Federal Sentencing Guidelines' exhortatory self-governance provisions enacted ten years earlier. Even Enron had a Code of Ethics.[34]

In response, Congress passed the Sarbanes-Oxley Act ("Sarbanes-Oxley") which—for the first time—required companies to establish codes of ethics or explain why they had not done so.[35] Sarbanes-Oxley originated with a series of Congressional hearings on the Enron collapse. Passage was expedited by the WorldCom fraud. The legislation was intended to restore confidence in U.S. capital markets. "The Sarbanes-Oxley Act is the most significant piece of corporate securities legislation since the Securities Act of 1933 and The Securities and Exchange Act of 1934. The Act's requirements are significant and have brought about substantial change in the work and role of auditors and the operations and financial disclosures of publicly traded corporations."[36] The Act mandates a new level of personal responsibility by requiring the CEO and CFO to personally certify the company's financial statements and disclosures, subject to fines and imprisonment for misrepresentation. More disclosure is required for certain transactions. The effectiveness of internal controls must be assessed and reported. Boards of directors must establish audit committees comprised of independent directors who will hire and oversee the external auditor.

What You See Is What You Get

What effect did Sarbanes-Oxley have on UTC? Many companies found the costs to implement Sarbanes-Oxley burdensome, substantially exceeding original estimates.[37] However, Sarbanes-Oxley compliance, to those companies which had fully implemented the DII principles, did not introduce radically new concepts and was not overly burdensome; the principles of openness, disclosure, self-reporting of violations, and senior management accountability were already embedded in their corporate cultures. UTC held its annual shareholders' meeting that year in the New York Public Library. In that meeting, George David told the shareholders that UTC aspired to be like the library, one of the truly open institutions of the world, and that with UTC's financial statements, "What you see is what you get."[38]

In 2004, amendments to the Federal Sentencing Guidelines brought further convergence with the DII principles first enunciated in 1986. The original focus of the guidelines was to encourage prevention and detection of criminal conduct, but the 2004 amendments expanded the scope to include promotion "of an organizational culture that encourages ethical conduct and a commitment to compliance with the law."[39] This amendment recognized that a proscriptive approach alone is less effective than an ethical organizational culture as a determinant of successful implementation of a compliance program.

Another 2004 amendment to the Sentencing Guidelines introduced specific requirements of risk assessment and periodic program evaluation. These new provisions require the company to collect performance data concerning its compliance and ethics program, such as:

1. Does the program effectively assess the actual risks the organization confronts, and the strengths and weaknesses of the organizational culture?

2. Does the program explicitly define expected outcomes?

3. Does the company allocate sufficient resources to the compliance and ethics program?

4. Does the company measure program effectiveness to confirm that it is making progress toward program goals?[40]

Questions

1. Can the continuous improvement methods of UTC's ACE system, which were developed primarily for a production environment, be effectively adapted to the Ethics and Compliance Program, a non-production program group?

2. How would the company measure attributes such as quality, on-time delivery, customer satisfaction, employee satisfaction, and productivity within the Ethics and Compliance Program?

3. How do you define program success for the Ethics and Compliance Program?

4. How should a company measure the commitment of management to an ethics program?

Sustaining an Ethical Culture

UTC's leadership states that an ethical culture, characterized by good communication, modeling ethical behavior, keeping commitments, and maintaining accountability, is good business. "The purpose of business is obtaining a fair return on investment. If you don't believe that you will obtain a fair return, then you will not invest. Investment thus is built on a belief that commitments will be kept—on the basis of mutuality—and frequently on the basis of mutual dependence."[41] Committed to ethics as the foundation of its consistent high performance, UTC was determined that its Ethics and Compliance Program would not become complacent and in 2004 launched a major effort to revitalize and strengthen the program. Not surprisingly for a company as process-driven as UTC, the company approached this effort as a business process management and problem-solving challenge. The first step was to gather data. For that, the company collaborated with the Ethics Resource Center, which had been collecting employee survey data periodically for ten years.

The Ethics Resource Center ("ERC") conducted its first National Business Ethics Survey® ("NBES") in 1994.[42] UTC and certain other DII members collaborated with the ERC to fine-tune the NBES survey questions for the defense industry and participated in the NBES 2005 and 2008 surveys, using the 2005 results as a baseline for ethics and compliance performance measurements.[43] The ERC's data from 1994 forward, including the 2005 data, suggested that stronger ethics and compliance program structure supported stronger ethical culture, and better outcomes were built on stronger ethical cultures. Consequently, to achieve better outcomes, the company should strengthen its program structure and its ethical culture. The elements of the ethics and compliance program structure included codes of conduct, ethics and compliance training, risk-management, audit, investigation, corrective action, and organizations responsible for oversight. Ethical culture was defined to mean how people behaved as indicated through survey questions focusing on behavior. UTC targeted four outcomes for improvement: (a) employee observations of violations of company's code; (b) pressure to commit violations; (c) unwillingness to report violations; (d) fear of retaliation for reporting violations ("Outcomes").

The ERC's analysis of the results of the 1994 survey and confirmation by the results of subsequent surveys supported the conclusion that four behaviors are the principal drivers for better Outcomes: (a) good communication concerning ethics; (b) modeling ethical behaviors; (c) keeping commitments; (d) maintaining accountability among all employees. UTC undertook a thorough series of improvements throughout its ethics and compliance activities keeping in mind the behaviors to be encouraged in support of better Outcomes. Then, in 2006, UTC initiated two fairly dramatic structural changes. First, an "Ethics Competency" was defined and incorporated into the performance metrics of all salaried employees. All performance competencies at UTC are rated by the degree to which the employee demonstrates the desired behaviors; the new Ethics Competency incorporates the behaviors previously identified as supporting better Outcomes by requiring demonstration of (a) good communication regarding ethics; (b) modeling ethical behaviors; (c) keeping commitments; (d) maintaining accountability among all employees; (e) visibly supporting the Ethics and Compliance Program; and (f) performing consistently with compliance mandates. Second, the company developed a set of "President's Ethics Objectives," designed to be applicable to the business unit Presidents, and flowed down to executives and managers; the "President's Ethics Objectives" require (a) communicating the importance of ethics; (b) providing ethics training to all employees; (c) identifying and mitigating compliance risks; (d) using process improvement tools to reduce compliance lapses and compliance losses; and (e) improving the score on the ethics category of UTC's Employee Engagement Survey. Performance to objectives is a critical factor in determining incentive compensation. It should be noted that none of the measurements associated with either the Ethics Competency or the Presidents' Ethics Objectives attempts to measure how ethical or unethical an employee may be. Rather, the measurements apply to actions and incentivize behaviors.

As described above, the DII companies who participated in the ERC survey used the 2005 results as a baseline and measured performance against the 2008 results. Between 2005 and 2008, UTC's score improved by 9 percentage points. Additionally, the biennial Employee Engagement Survey administered since 1999/2000, contains a module of seven ethics questions, four structural and three cultural. The ethics category in the survey was flat through 2005, but in 2007, two years after introducing the Ethics Competency and the Presidents' Ethics Objectives, the composite score in the ethics category improved by ten percentage points, and by another five points in 2009.

The structural changes UTC initiated in 2006 and the use of quantitative tools in support of program improvement were the focus of the 2010 Pace award, "for moving beyond words, by focusing also on systems and execution that make every employee responsible for meeting the company's ethical goals . . . (and) making ethical conduct a fundamental part of UTC's DNA."[44]

Looking toward the future, the 2011 NBES findings have identified certain trends which may affect companies like UTC and their ethics and compliance programs. The key findings are summarized as follows:

- Misconduct witnessed by U.S. workers is now at historic lows, while reporting of misconduct is now at near highs.

- Retaliation against employee whistleblowers rose sharply.

- The percentage of employees who perceived pressure to compromise standards in order to do their jobs climbed five points from 2009 to 13 percent.

- The share of companies with weak ethics cultures also climbed to near record levels.

- Two influences stood out in the unusual shift in trends: the economy and the unique experiences of those actively using social networking at work.

- NBES continues to show that companies behave differently during economic difficulties. The decisions and behaviors of their leaders are perceived by employees as a heightened commitment to ethics. As a result, employees adopt a higher standard of conduct for themselves.

- As the economy gets better—and companies and employees become more optimistic about their financial futures—it seems likely that misconduct will rise and reporting will drop, mirroring the growth in pressure and retaliation that have already taken place and conforming to historic patterns.

- Active social networkers report far more negative experiences in their workplaces. As a group, they are much more likely to experience pressure to compromise ethics standards and to experience retaliation for reporting misconduct than co-workers who are less involved with social networking.

- Active social networkers show a higher tolerance for certain activities that could be considered questionable.

- There may be an opportunity for corporations to work with active social networkers in ways that they have not yet fully explored. Active social networkers are somewhat more likely to use social networks to say positive things about their company and co-workers, than to post negative feelings.

Questions

1. What types of employee surveys are useful for evaluating an ethics program?

2. Can a survey accurately measure what actions employees will take under certain circumstances? For example, a survey might ask employees if they would call the hotline to report misconduct by a fellow employee; how reliable would the responses to that question be?

3. Can a survey accurately measure general employee attitudes through the "agree–disagree" type of questions?

4. How can companies measure the effectiveness of ethics training?

5. How might the company measure employee skepticism regarding corporate assurances of confidentially and non-retaliation?

6. Do the findings suggest any issues that may affect UTC's Ethics and Compliance Program?

UTC Subsidiaries Plead Guilty to Export Violations

On June 28, 2012, Pratt & Whitney Canada Corp. ("PWC"), a Canadian subsidiary of UTC pleaded guilty to violating the Arms Export Control Act and making false statements in connection with its illegal export to China of U.S.-origin military software used in the development of China's first modern military attack helicopter, the Z-10. In addition, UTC and its subsidiaries PWC and Hamilton Sundstrand Corporation (HSC) agreed to pay more than $75 million as part of a global settlement with the Justice Department and State Department in connection with the China arms export violations and for making false and belated disclosures to the U.S. government about these illegal exports.[45]

Since 1989, the United States has embargoed export to China of all U.S. defense articles and associated technical data as a result of the conduct of China's military in Tiananmen Square. The embargo was codified in 1990 by Congressional prohibition on licensing technology to the PRC. PWC delivered ten development engines to

China in 2001 and 2002. Despite the military nature of the Z-10 helicopter, PWC determined on its own that these development engines for the Z-10 did not constitute "defense articles," requiring a U.S. export license, because they were identical to those engines PWC was already supplying China for a commercial helicopter.

Some individuals in PWC knew from the start of the Z-10 project in 2000 that the Chinese were developing an attack helicopter and that supplying it with U.S.-origin components would be illegal. When the Chinese claimed that a civil version of the helicopter would be developed in parallel, PWC marketing personnel expressed skepticism internally about the "sudden appearance" of the civil program, the timing of which they questioned as "real or imagined." PWC nevertheless saw an opening for PWC "to insist on exclusivity in [the] civil version of this helicopter," and stated that the Chinese would "no longer make reference to the military program." PWC failed to notify UTC or HSC about the attack helicopter until years later and purposely turned a blind eye to the helicopter's military application.[46]

> Pratt & Whitney executives also kept the military end-use of its engines and software secret from some of the company's engineers. When two were dispatched to China in March 2003 to observe the helicopters, one asked a Chinese official, "where are the other 10 seats," meaning those intended for civilian passengers? The helicopter they saw had only two seats in tandem—typical of an attack model—and mock weapons on the hull. According to federal prosecutors who interviewed the engineers, the Chinese official smiled and said, in effect, that it had always been an attack helicopter.[47]

Upon their return to Montreal, the two engineers discussed their concerns with the company's manager for Asian marketing, but work on the project continued without constraints.

In February 2004 HSC terminated its participation in the project, having concluded that the intended use of its software was in fact military rather than commercial. PWC continued to work on the project. PWC developed its own software modifications and continued to export to China through June 2005.

In July 2006, UTC made a limited voluntary disclosure, and two supplemental disclosures in August and September 2006 to the State Department about the company's involvement in the China project. It appears that the internal investigation leading to the voluntary disclosure was triggered by an institutional investor's inquiry. It is perhaps a warning flag that UTC's own internal processes did not reveal the improprieties. In addition, the July voluntary disclosure itself contained false statements, asserting that the company did not know of the intended military application of the technology until approximately 2003–2004. According to the Department of Justice court documents conclusively demonstrated that the company knew of the intended use at the beginning of the project in 2000.[48] In addition to the monetary fines, UTC is subject to special government oversight for at least two years. UTC has also taken corrective actions to formalize certain processes and elevate scrutiny of its international trade functions.

Questions

1. What elements of UTC's Code of Ethics applied to the actions and decisions which eventually resulted in the 2012 guilty pleas?

2. Were those actions and decisions indicative of systemic weaknesses in UTC's ethical culture or were they anomalies?

3. How might UTC have identified the problem and prevented the regrettable outcome?

Endnotes

1. "HOME > OUR COMPANY: KEY FACTS." *United Technologies Corporation,* accessed December 21, 2014. http://www.utc.com/Our-Company/Pages/Key-Facts.aspx.

2. "United Technologies Corp. and CEO Louis Chênevert Win ERC's 2010 Pace Award for Leadership in Business Ethics." *Ethics Resource Center.* http://www.ethics.org/news/united-technologies-corp-and-ceo-louis-chênevert-win-erc's-2010-pace-award-leadership-business-

3. Ibid.

4. U.S. House of Representatives, Committee on the Judiciary, *Major Fraud Act of 1988, Hearings.* (Washington D.C.: GPO, 1989), 122–125.

5. U.S. House of Representatives, Committee on the Judiciary. *Role of Whistleblowers in Administrative Proceedings, Hearings.* (Washington D.C.: GPO, 1983), 8.

6. U.S. Department of Justice. *Justice Department Sues United Technologies Division for Overcharges on Jet Engine Contract.* http://www.justice.gov/opa/pr/1999/March/075civ.htm

7. U.S. Department of Justice. *UTC Pays $14.8 Million to Settle Military Aid Complaint.* http://www.justice.gov/opa/pr/1997/May97/211civ.htm.

8. Major Fraud Act of 1988, Hearings. (Statement of the U.S. Chamber of Commerce), 198–205.

9. The President's Blue Ribbon Commission on Defense Management. *A Quest For Excellence: Final Report to the President by the President's Blue Ribbon Commission on Defense Management.* 1986. See p. 78 and Appendix M.

10. See e.g., Fritz, Sara. "Senate Votes Restrictions on Defense Firms." *LA Times,* May 1985.

11. U.S. House of Representatives, Committee on the Judiciary. *GAO Efforts Related to Fraud, Abuse and Mismanagement in Federal Programs.* (Washington D.C.: GPO, 1979), 8.

12. U.S. Department of Defense, Office of Inspector General. *Indicators of Fraud in DoD Procurement.* U.S. Government Printing Office, 1987. Print.

13. Cox, Timothy. "Is the Procurement Integrity Act 'Important' Enough for the Mandatory Inclusion rule? A Case for Inclusion." *Public Contract Law Journal.* http://pclj.org/volume-40.

14. Office of the President. *Executive Order 12526—President's Blue Ribbon Commission on Defense Management,* 1985.

15. Packard Commission Final Report to the President, pp. 75–89 and Appendix M.

16. Defense Industry Initiative on Business Ethics and Conduct. "Who We Are." http://www.dii.org/about-us.

17. United Technologies Corporation. *Policy Statement—Business Ethics and Conduct in Contracting with the United States Government.* Hartford, CT, 2006. Allegations of fraud, waste, and abuse continued to surface from UTC's defense industry business units for some time. E.g.: U.S. Department of Justice. *Sikorsky Aircraft Pays $2.9 Million to Settle False Claims Act Allegations.* https://www.google.com/search?client=safari&rls=en&q=U.S.+Department+of+Justice+Sikorsky-+Aircraft+Pays+$2.9+Million+to+Settle+False+Claims+Act+Allegations&ie=UTF-8&oe=UTF-8 (relating to claims from 1991 to 2006); U.S. Department of Justice. *Justice Department Sues United Technologies Division for Overcharges on Jet Engine Contract.* http://www.justice.gov/archive/opa/pr/1999/March/075civ.htm (alleging $75 million in overcharges from 1985 to 1991).

18. Desio, Paula. United States Sentencing Commission. *An Overview of the Organizational Guidelines.* http://www.ussc.gov/sites/default/files/pdf/training/organizational-guidelines/ORGOVERVIEW.pdf.

19. Ethics Resource Center. "The Federal Sentencing Guidelines for Organizations at Twenty Years." http://www.ethics.org/page/fsgo-federal-sentencing-guidelines-organizations-20-years.

20. United States Sentencing Commission. Guidelines Manual. http://www.ussc.gov/guidelines-manual/2014/2014-ussc-guidelines-manual.

21. Ibid.

22. Ethics Resource Center. *The Federal Sentencing Guidelines for Organizations at Twenty Years.*

23. United Technologies Corporation. "At A Glance" http://www.utc.com/Our-Businesses/Pages/At-A-Glance.aspx#bis. (2015).

24. Brady, Diane. "The Unsung CEO: United Technologies' CEO George David runs a $31 billion company that outguns GE in shareholder return. Who is he—and how does he do it?" *Bloomberg Business Week.* October 24, 2004. http://www.businessweek.com/stories/2004-10-24/the-unsung-ceo.

25. The UTC Code of Ethics is available in thirty-eight languages. United Technologies Corporation. *Code of Ethics.* http://www.utc.com/Our-Company/Ethics-And-Compliance/Pages/Code-of-Ethics.aspx.

26. At maturity, UTC's Code of Ethics would embrace diversity without compromising the fundamental principles of its ethics code: "UTC is a global company serving markets worldwide, often doing business under laws, cultural norms, and socials standards that differ widely across regions and countries. UTC will abide by the national and local laws of the countries in which we operate. If a conflict arises with respect to laws applicable between countries, the Legal Department must be consulted. UTC will not knowingly facilitate illegal conduct or fraud by others, regardless of local norms." United Technologies Corporation. Code of Ethics. http://www.utc.com/StaticFiles/UTC/StaticFiles/coe_english.pdf.

27. Ibid. Information in the remainder of this section was obtained from the UTC Code of Ethics.

28. United Technologies Corporation. *Shareowner Letter, 2013 Annual Report.* http://2013ar.utc.com/letter_shareowner.htm.

29. Brady, "The Unsung CEO."

30. Roth, George. United Technologies Corporation: Achieving Competitive Excellence (ACE): Operating System Case Study. http://hdl.handle.net/1721.1/81998.

31. Brady, "The Unsung CEO."

32. Ackman, Dan. "WorldCom, Tyco, Enron—R.I.P." *Forbes.* July 1, 2002. http://www.forbes.com/2002/07/01/0701topnews.html.

33. Ethics Resource Center. *The Federal Sentencing Guidelines for Organizations at Twenty Years.*

34. The Smoking Gun. *Enron's Code of Ethics.* http://www.thesmokinggun.com/file/enrons-code-ethics?page=1.

35. Keogh, Kevin. White & Case. "Thanks to SOX, You Need COE for Your CEO and CFO." http://www.whitecase.com/Publications/Detail.aspx?publication=438#.VMJh98ZbqS2.

36. Keating, Elizabeth and The Corporate Governance and Accountability Project Team. "Teaching Note for Sarbanes-Oxley Act: What Has it Wrought?" The Aspen Institute Center for Business Education. http://www.caseplace.org/d.asp?d=2812.

37. Ibid., p. 7.

38. McClenahen, John S. "UTC's Master of Principle." *IndustryWeek*. Dec. 21, 2004. http://www.industryweek.com/articles/utcs_master_of_principle_1195.aspx.

39. United States Sentencing Commission. Guidelines Manual. http://www.ussc.gov/guidelines-manual/2014/2014-ussc-guidelines-manual.

40. Johnson, Kenneth W. "Federal Sentencing Guidelines: Key Points and Profound Changes." Ethics Resource Center FSGO Series. Part 1. http://www.ethics.org/resource/fsgo-series-part-1.

41. Monts, Michael. Remarks concerning ethics and compliance. Remarks presented at the Singapore Business Federation, Singapore, March 31, 2006 http://utc.com/News/Archive/2006/Singapore+Business+Federation+Singapore

42. Ethics Resource Center. "2011 National Business Ethics Survey®." http://ethics.org/files/u5/FinalNBES-web_0.pdf.

43. Monts, Michael. "Using Program Structure to Improve Ethical Performance: Applying the Research Findings of the Ethics Resource Center." 2010. Print. Presentation to the PLI Compliance and Ethics Institute. Information for the remainder of this section was obtained from the PLI presentation.

44. "Pace Award." *Ethics Resource Center.*

45. U.S. Department of Justice. *United Technologies Subsidiary Pleads Guilty to Criminal Charges for Helping China Develop New Attack Helicopter: United Technologies, Pratt & Whitney Canada and Hamilton Sundstrand Corporation Also Agree to Pay More Than $75 Million to U.S. Government.* http://www.justice.gov/opa/pr/2012/June/12-nsd-824.html.

46. Toombs, Zach, and R. Jeffrey Smith. "Pentagon Contractor Caught Illegally Selling Military Technology to China." *The Atlantic.* July 6, 2012. Information for the remainder of this section was obtained from the Toombs and Smith article. http://www.theatlantic.com/international/archive/2012/07/pentagon-contractor-caught-illegally-selling-military-technology-to-china/259469/

47. Ibid.

48. Department of Justice. *United Technologies Subsidiary Pleads Guilty.*

CHAPTER 6

Simulation Supplement:
Chapter 3
Additional Facts and Issues

The supplemental facts and issues in this chapter can be introduced during the simulated Board of Directors' meetings. Each of the supplements is based on the author's real-world experiences as a corporate attorney. One measure of simulation effectiveness is how closely the simulation replicates the real world. The Chapter 3 exercises are intended to be realistic, down to the parameters of not enough time and not enough money. The supplements add to the mix the quality of disruption, challenging the students' ability to be agile and flexible while they solve problems. To address the issues they must work together, share information, and reach agreements despite conflicts from conflicting objectives. The supplements can be introduced in 15-minute intervals.

CHAPTER ORGANIZATION

Session 1: The Founders—4-member team

No supplement

Session 1: The Founders—5-member team

No supplement

Session 2: The Investigation—4-member team

Additional Facts

Mr. Goodwrench

Four people are in your office. They have government identification and badges. One of them says he is from the Department of Homeland Security (your government contract customer), Office of the Inspector General, and he is wearing a gun. They say they have been informed of a dangerous toxic spill at this site and are here to investigate. They wish to speak to you immediately. What are your instructions?

Mr. Wizard

Security says a news crew with cameras is outside the building, on the sidewalk. They want to come in and interview you. They are positioned near the cafeteria exit from which the employees will be leaving in 20 minutes. A breaking news segment is on the air already, on local broadcast channels, interrupting regular programming and stating that they have been informed by one of the workers who has asked to remain anonymous that there has been a toxic spill, releasing fumes into the air and toxic waste into the aquifer, and an unknown number of employees have been injured. You have ordered security to lock the cafeteria exit door. What are your instructions?

Session 2: The Investigation—5-member team

Additional Facts

Mr. Donaghy

Four people are in your office. They have government identification and badges. One of them says he is from the Department of Homeland Security (your government contract customer), Office of the Inspector General, and he is wearing a gun. They say they have been informed of a dangerous toxic spill at this site and are here to investigate. They wish to speak to you immediately. What are your instructions?

Mr. Wizard

Security says a news crew with cameras is on the sidewalk at the front of the building. They want to come in and interview you. They are near the exit from which the employees will be leaving in 20 minutes. A breaking news segment is on the air already, on local broadcast channels. The broadcast is interrupting regular programming and stating that they have been informed by one of the workers who has asked to remain anonymous that there has been a toxic spill, releasing fumes into the air and toxic waste into the aquifer and an unknown number of employees has been injured. You have ordered security to lock the exit door. What are your instructions?

Session 3: Goodbye Yellow Brick Road—4-member team

Additional Facts

Mr. Goodwrench

The outside auditors have asked for an emergency meeting with you. They have discovered that Mr. Money-penny is falsifying charges on his expense reports, and funding home improvements at his house on the company charge card. Charges include a hot tub (with jets and pulsating, multicolored lights), wine and beer in the amount of $8,437.62, and a yellow Vespa.

Ms. Winfrey

Two agents from the Homeland Security Office of the Inspector General are in the lobby. They wish to speak with you immediately about certain allegations that have come to their attention concerning unlawful age discrimination occurring at this company, in violation of the law and of the terms of the government contracts to which the company is a party. They are in possession of certain emails that substantiate their allegations. They say that if you do not cooperate, they will execute a search warrant and seize all the company's documents, including mobile hard drives and mobile devices. What are your instructions?

Session 3: Goodbye Yellow Brick Road—5-member team

Additional Facts

Mr. Goodwrench

The outside auditors have asked for an emergency meeting with you. They have discovered that Mr. Moneypenny is falsifying charges on his expense reports, and funding home improvements at his house on the company charge card. Charges include a hot tub (with jets and pulsating, multicolored lights), wine and beer in the amount of $8,437.62, and a yellow Vespa.

© Ruslan Grumble/Shutterstock

Ms. Winfrey

Two agents from the Homeland Security Office of the Inspector General are in the lobby. They wish to speak with you immediately about certain allegations that have come to their attention concerning unlawful age discrimination occurring at this company, in violation of the law and of the terms of the government contracts to which the company is a party. They are in possession of certain emails that substantiate their allegations. They say that if you do not cooperate, they will execute a search warrant and seize all the company's documents, including mobile hard drives and mobile devices. What are your instructions?

Session 4: How Do You Sleep at Night?—4-member team

Mr. Moneypenny

You have been reviewing your folder on the Crawford matter, including her withholdings elections, when you realize something awful: Ms. Crawford is a single mother of four. She holds down a second job cleaning other peoples' houses. Furthermore, according to an informal note your staff slipped into your folder, in order to feed her children she gets food stamps and gets her groceries at the local food bank. You are horrified. You assert—forcefully and emotionally—that any decision about Ms. Crawford should take this information into account.

Session 4: How Do You Sleep at Night?—5-member team

Mr. Moneypenny

You have been reviewing your folder on the Crawford matter, including her withholdings elections, when you realize something awful: Ms. Crawford is a single mother of four. She holds down a second job cleaning other peoples' houses. Furthermore, according to an informal note your staff slipped into your folder, in order to feed her children she gets food stamps and gets her groceries at the local food bank. You are horrified. You assert—forcefully and emotionally—that any decision about Ms. Crawford should take this information into account.

CPSIA information can be obtained at www.ICGtesting.com
Printed in the USA
BVOW09s1040250816

459950BV00008B/71/P